1965 Shelby GT350R Clone

Quote from my younger brother Bill ...

"We both have gasoline in our veins Michael ... however that is where the similarity ends.

I have a normal heart, yours has eight f__king cylinders!"

1968 Greenwood Corvette

BIKER TALES

...and we don't eat our young!

MICHAEL E. MURRAY

Sports Car Driver . Real Estate Broker . Auctioneer . Artist . Author . Biker

My life in short stories, I hope you live your life to the fullest as I did

PREFACE

For as long as I can remember, people have been saying to me, Michael you should write a book about your exciting life. Clever idea but … I did not have a clue about how to do it until I heard Jack Canfield, author of Chicken Soup for the Soul in the mid-nineties. He was the keynote speaker at a Floyd Wickman Master Sales Academy real estate convention in Las Vegas. I loved that book so much I read a story from the book every week at my sales meetings to my team at the Danberry Real Estate Company in Toledo, Ohio.

Bling! The light bulb went off. Great idea I just did not have enough stories yet. Thirty years later I started authoring my stories. Each adventure I had; I wrote as a short story. I live by, "If you invite me, I will come". You never know who you will meet or what adventures lay ahead.

My many adventures include my early childhood growing up with seven siblings: my pin striping art, sign painting, professional sports car racing, real estate career, politics, motorcycling and world travels.

"Drive it like you stole it"!

I hope that enjoy them. You will laugh and you will cry.

TABLE OF CONTENTS

CHAPTER 1

A Chance Meeting

I saw my neighbor and friend Brigelle Thomas at the grocery store this afternoon. She is a wonderful mother of seven children. It brought back memories of my childhood growing up with seven siblings. I wrote her this message.

Dear Brigelle,

It was nice running into you and the children at the store today. It brought back memories of my childhood.

My dad was a milkman and delivered milk with a horse and wagon for the Sealtest Dairy. He was paid every Friday. Friday evening after super, my mother went grocery shopping. My dad made $100 a week. He gave mom $50 for groceries.

One of us would go along and choose the flavor of soda that was divided into ten cups to drink with the large bowl of popcorn she made that evening. We watched TV shows and ate popcorn on the black and white TV my grandma Murray bought us.

Mom squirreled away a dollar a week for her Christmas club account to make sure we had one gift under the tree at Christmas.

My oldest sister Ann, worked on Saturdays at the Anderson Bakery around the corner on Spencer St.in Toledo, Ohio. A dozen donuts was forty-eight cents. She bought a dozen donuts for our Sunday breakfast for 24 cents with her employee discount.

Thank you for bringing back these memories.

Michael

CHAPTER 2

No Love at Home

This is the most painful chapter I will write. I went through therapy in my mid-40s. I had gone through two marriages and was seeking answers. A family therapist started by asking me questions about my childhood. I had few memories. Little did I know I was opening the door to the worst emotional pain a person could feel.

Susie Shew, my therapist, had me interview my seven siblings to see what their memories were. I needed to find the pieces to the puzzle of my lost memories from my childhood. I had few memories. Little did I know I was opening the door to the worst emotional pain a person could feel. We were all abused emotionally and several of us physically. We did not get spankings; we got beatings. I was the third oldest of eight children, a middle child. My mother had six children in a row, then eight years later had two more. There was no love and affection for me. My parents were very cold. Children find ways to survive abuse. My older sister and brother became perfect. I put up an emotional wall. I had no deep feelings.

I also found out two deep secrets. We suppress painful memories. I was a bed wetter until about 10 years old. I also sat up in bed in my sleep and rocked back and forth until my mid-teens. I was blown away when my oldest sister shared these memories of my childhood. I went right to Susie, my therapist, and asked why I rocked the bed in my sleep. She explained that I was nurturing myself since I was not nurtured by my parents. After these revelations, I could not work or eat well for six months. These pieces to my puzzle were devastating. I was an emotional wreck.

I was having lunch with a doctor friend. He noticed I was barely eating a bowl of soup. I had lost 27 pounds. He asked what was wrong. I shared my story with him. After lunch, I followed him back to his office for a script for an antidepressant.

My life changed when at nineteen, I met Karen (sixteen). I came out of my shell and fell head over heels in love. My heart was pumping, I could not eat or sleep. WOW! It was exciting. She was the oldest of nine. It gets better. Her mother Francis … for the first time I felt a mother's love. This lasted for one year until she went off to college. One day I received the dear Michael letter. No reason given.

I was heartbroken. It was devastating. I packed a bag and drove my Shelby GT350 eight hours to Maryville, Missouri. I needed to know what happened. We had supper together that night and the truth came out. It was a fraternity guy.

I stayed in a motel near the campus that night. We planned on breakfast the next morning. I cried myself to sleep. I woke up about 3 a.m., packed my bag and drove home. I did not show up for breakfast the next morning.

I chose not to stay in touch with her family. It would have been too painful. I lost two loves that day. Karen and her mom. I returned to my shell.

Two years later, Karen and I got back together. My love and deep feelings were still there. I was so in love. We decided to get married the summer before her senior year. I owned my own business and was able to provide a good living for us. We checked a local college, Mary Manse, in Toledo, where she could finish college.

Her parents said no. They wanted her to finish college in Missouri. I could not blame them. We eventually went separate ways. I returned to my safe place, my shell. I pined for 10 years. Day in and day out for 10 years. I did not know how to move on.

Three years later, I heard Karen was getting married. I was racing sports cars at the time. I was on my way to Indianapolis for a sports car race. It was my first year of racing. I needed to finish this race for it to count for my Sports Car Club of America competition license. I was driving my tow truck and trailer through Maumee, Ohio, and drove by St. Joseph's Catholic Church. I saw her father's yellow Chrysler all decorated in front of the church. It hit me like a ton of bricks. I cried all the way to Indy. Once I got to the racetrack, I drove my Shelby GT350 Mustang into the ground. The engine overheated and blew up. My heart was broken; I was hurting and angry. I went through two marriages looking for love. It was not that they didn't love me; I did not come out of my safe shell and allow myself to love deeply again.

Ten years later, I was Christmas shopping at the mall and bumped into Francis. I could still feel her warm love for me. Just her presence conveyed her mother's love for me. That evening a weight was lifted off my shoulders and I was able to let go and stop pining.

I saw Francis again at her husband's funeral about eight years ago. As she was exiting the funeral service, she saw me and winked. I lit up. She was in her mid-80s. I did not let this opportunity slip by. Three or four times a year, I stopped in to visit with her. I always brought her chocolates. I still felt her motherly love. She was loved by all. She passed away several years ago. I will never forget Francis McCartney.

My therapy was successful thanks to Susie Shue. She was exceptionally good at moving me along on my journey. One year start to finish. The walls came down; I was able to love again.

The next Christmas, I had a dessert open house. I made 25 desserts from scratch. The invitation read, "Bring me an ornament for my tree and I'll feed you a dessert from around the world." Susie Shue's ornament was a silver star. Her note read, "Michael you are a bright shining star, few people start therapy and fewer finish."

**My brothers and sisters. Top Jim, Ann, Terry, Michael
Bottom Mary, Patty, Bill, Dave**

CHAPTER 3

Growing Up at Home

My parents' house payment was $52 a month back in the 50s. We had nothing; there were no extras; we each had one pair of shoes. I wore my brother Jim's hand-me-down clothes and shoes; my brother Terry wore my hand-me-downs. There were no after-school snacks; nothing to eat after supper, and you did not dare raid the refrigerator. We did have a clean house and clean clothes. If you did not make your bed, there was no dessert with supper. To this day I make my bed daily.

We lived in a three-bedroom house at 744 Nicholas St.in Toledo's south end neighborhood with one bathroom. Five boys in one bedroom and three girls in the another. Dad would not give us a nickel for anything; do not bother to ask. We cut grass with a push mower and shoveled snow for neighbors whenever we had the chance to try and earn some extra money. I went to bed hungry most often.

When I earned a quarter, I rode my bike to Acme drugs at South and Spencer Streets in Toledo's south end. I bought a vanilla milkshake to fill my stomach. I had a weekly baby-sitting job when I was 12 on Saturday nights for Ms. Yost's son Gary. The going rate was 25 cents an hour, but she usually gave me 50 cents an hour. A dollar would buy four milkshakes.

The magazine rack was behind my swivel seat in the ice cream parlor part of the drug store. I read hot rod magazines while drinking a milkshake and dreaming about cool cars. The famous pinstriping artist Von Dutch from California sold pin-striping decals through hot rod magazines. I was into building model cars and customizing them. I copied Von Dutch's designs with a brush I cut down so I could paint the small designs on my model hot rods. I then graduated to pinstriping bicycles. If you owned a bicycle and lived in my neighborhood, I pinstriped for free.

CHAPTER 4

Earning My Independence

One Christmas I was four or five and was quarantined to my bed upstairs because I was contagious with chicken pox. My rich Aunt Katie and Uncle Bill came over with presents for us. I remember crying because I could not go downstairs. Then I heard Aunt Katie ask my dad, "Where's Michael?" He told her that I was upstairs because I had chicken pox and could not come downstairs because I was contagious. She came upstairs and picked me up and carried me downstairs and gave me my present. She held me all evening and put me to bed later. I loved my dear Aunt Katie. I still get emotional when I have this memory.

My father was never in the military, but he ran his house like a marine drill sergeant. With eight children and one bathroom he would call out our names from the oldest to the youngest. We each had five minutes in the bathroom in the morning. Baths were at night. Mom was downstairs in the kitchen making breakfast and packing lunches. You made your bed or no dessert at supper. You left no dirty clothes on the floor. Supper was at 5:30 sharp. Only one person could speak at a time. You ate everything you were given whether you liked it or not. I hated beets and had to sit there until I ate them all. On Sunday we would march single file into church, the youngest first and the oldest last. We were expected to never disrespect Mom, Dad, or others.

On Christmas we received one small gift from Santa. My grandma Murray always bought us a five-dollar membership to the Catholic Club. On Saturdays I took a bus or hitchhiked to the Catholic Club on 16th Street in downtown Toledo. I went swimming, played basketball, and hung out in the woodworking shop. One day I had a bright idea to make a shoeshine box. Tom's Barber Shop was on the corner and the Murray family were regulars. I had no idea how to shine shoes. My dad spotted me a few bucks for black, brown and Cordovan shoe polish, a stiff brush, and a buffing rag. He showed me how to do get a good shine. One Saturday I stopped in and asked Tom if I could shine shoes every Saturday. I charged ten cents a shine. WOW, my first real job at 12 years old. On a good day I could make a dollar so I could buy a milkshake for four days and read the hot rod magazines.

Before Grandma Murray bought us our first TV, Mom would let us boys take the radio to our bedroom on Saturday nights. We fell asleep listening to Batman, Gene Autry and my fav, The Lone Ranger.

I traded in my shoeshine box when I bought my brother Jim's paper route on our street. In those days you had to buy the route for a dollar a customer. I had 84 customers on the three blocks on Nicholas Street. I made weekly payments to Jim until the route was paid for.

Every day after school I rode my bike to the Toledo *Blade* station at Carlton and Spencer Streets. I learned the art of pitching pennies against the wall while waiting for papers to arrive. Closest to wall won. A perfect day of delivering papers was when every throw made it on the porch. If you missed you stopped, parked your bike, and put the paper on the porch. If you have a job, do it right. Every Saturday morning, I went door to door to collect my route. *The Blade* was 48 cents a week. When Christmas came around most customers gave me 50 cents or a dollar tip. I was now financially independent. I also vowed that my children would never be hungry like I was.

CHAPTER 5

My Nickname

All the Murray kids went to St. James Catholic Elementary School at Orchard and Broadway Streets in old South Toledo. The tuition was $25 for the first child, $15 for the second, five for the third, and the rest were free. My dad made out well. For several years there were six of us attending St. James.

In the seventh grade my older brother Jim and I played football for the school team. He was big Murray, and I was little Murray. Eighth grade, seventh grade together. I played right guard; Jim was left. Fritz Kunz was the quarterback and Tutti Ferguson was the fullback. Before and after practice we ran laps to warm up, get in shape or cool down. Our coach and Boy Scout Master was Okie Woods, a Jeep employee by day. Coach said I ran like a duck, so I had to run laps backwards. Coach Woods named me "Duck Foot." My friends me called Duck for short. I was cool! I wore the name proudly. Other boys were named Junior, Buddy, or Mac. I still see Fritz Kunz at Cars & Coffee with his 308 Ferrari. Wayne "Tutti" Ferguson died incredibly young.

My pinstriping idol was Von Dutch; my artist pen name became Von Duck. I proudly signed the bicycles I pinstriped Von Duck.

When I was 15 and a first-year student at Central Catholic High School, I played CYO basketball for St. James on weekends. Saturday morning was practice at Westminster Gym in downtown Toledo. One day as I crossed Spencer Street to catch a bus for basketball practice, I saw a sign painter, Dave Quinn, painting a sign on the window at the "Round Up Cafe" a greasy spoon on the corner that made delicious burgers, fries, and milkshakes. I walked over and watched in awe! I could not believe my eyes. Car names were becoming the latest hot rod craze and I wanted to learn how to do hand lettering. I knew I could make a buck lettering car names on cool cars. My parents tried to discourage me from becoming an artist. They said I would starve. I did not listen and was going to prove them wrong. I was following my heart and was not going to be sidetracked.

Dave was truly kind to this young kid. He said there were no schools around here that taught sign painting but there was a young man named Wally who owned the Wally Sign Company on Monroe at 16th Street who might teach me art. I was an art major at Central Catholic High School, so this new endeavor fit right in. I had the passion and was eager to learn.

Monday after school I went and met Wally Delvaux and became the shop boy. It was a two-mile walk from Central Catholic High School to Wally's. Sometimes I would hitchhike, so I could get there quicker. My job started by sweeping the floors, cleaning the silk screens, and coating out wooden signs that Wally hand lettered. I soon became his apprentice and joined the sign painter's union LU 546. I made $1.10 an hour.

Wally was my first mentor. I owe a tremendous amount of gratitude to him for taking me under his wing and becoming my friend and teacher about life, art, and business. He taught me layout, color, how to manage a brush and many alphabets. When I was sixteen and had my driver's license, I drove his VW pickup truck to Sherwin Williams paint store at Swayne Field on Monroe Street to pick up our paint supplies. My dad taught us how to drive and get our license. After that we were not allowed to use his car. Do not even ask to borrow dad's car. My method of transportation was bike, bus, or hitchhike.

After work and on Saturdays, I practiced my lettering. I was not good enough to paint for our customers, but Wally helped and let me freelance on my own. My side hustle was lettering car names and pinstriping hot rods.

One day Bob Lusher from Lusher Auto Parts in Walbridge, Ohio, called and said he heard I was a surprisingly good sign painter. I agreed (LOL). He needed the numbers painted on his new stock car. He asked if could do it the following Saturday and started giving me directions. I told him I was not old enough to drive and he would have to pick me up.

He picked me up early the following Saturday and I saw my first junkyard. Oh my! There was an old building with a dirt floor and a freshly painted bright orange race car inside. My little sign kit was an old makeup box my oldest sister, Ann, gave me. He left me alone and I went to work. I drew the numbers with a white Stabilo pencil and started painting.

About noon he came in and said, "Kid, are you hungry?" I said, "Yes, sir." Bob complimented me on my work. He drove us to Earl Cousino's Steak House (my Central buddy and good friend Thomas Cousino's father's restaurant) on Fassett and Miami Streets in East Toledo. Bob Lusher was a BIG man who wore bib overalls… He ordered T-bone steak dinners with all trimmings for us. When the server served our steaks on sizzling hot iron platters he said, "Honey, bring us two more." I was in awe! Two steak dinners for lunch! The only steak I had ever eaten was mom's fried cubed round steak with gravy on mashed potatoes. I could not wait to tell my siblings I had two steak dinners for lunch, and I made $25 for the day.

CHAPTER 6

Central vs. St. Francis 1960

I dug deep for this one. When I was a sophomore at Central Catholic High School, the home of the Fighting Irish, we were playing the St. Francis Knights for the first time in Toledo city league football.

Central was a coed school and along came St. Francis, an all-boy's Catholic high school. Their first senior class was 1960 and the rivalry began. The schools co-designed a beautiful trophy about three-foot-tall of a knight in shining armor and partially painted "Irish" green. The trophy was named the Irish Knight. I was a young sign painter, an art major and had a good grasp for laying out large letters.

Jim Nicholson, Gordy Capshaw, and I scaled the stone fence at Toledo University's football stadium in the middle of the night before the game. We brought 10-pound bags of flour and I went to work. I started at the middle of the field and drew a huge shamrock about 40–50 feet in diameter with flour. At one end of the field in six-foot letters, I wrote "Go Irish" and at the other end "CCHS" (Central Catholic High School).

We got out of there without getting caught. Next day we went to the big game and watched the groundskeepers trying to erase my art with brooms. It did not work to well because the dew on the grass hardened the flour. We laughed our butts off.

St. Francis won 20–8.

CHAPTER 7

My First Real Adventure

My Tom Sawyer adventure and my first international trip ... when I was 16 years old. I met Rob Roberts through my good friend Gordon Capshaw. Rob was 19, a beatnik (we had beatniks before there were hippies) and drove a beautiful British racing green Morgan roadster. He lived on River Road close to the Maumee, Ohio, border near the train tracks. His parents owned a 24-foot pontoon raft with an 18 horsepower Evinrude engine and docked it at the Maumee River Yacht Club.

He had been planning a raft trip to Leamington, Ontario, Canada, across Lake Erie, and camping on the beach at Point Pelee provincial park. Rob was having a tough time finding someone to go with him. He asked me, and I was in, but I had to ask my mother first. I was very independent because I had been on my own financially since I was 12. Oh, I had curfews, had to get good grades, and stay on the straight and narrow path (wink, wink). I knew better than to ask my dad. Mom said it be okay with her if it was okay with the Coast Guard. So, I called from a phone booth near Acme Drugs on South Street. I knew better than to call from home. The Coast Guard said if we catch you on Lake Erie in one of those pontoon rafts, we will tow you in. Yes, sir! Mom, the Coast Guard said it was okay.

Now the planning began. I was working at Wally Sign Company. We had four empty five-gallon thinner cans behind the shop. The raft had a five-gallon gas tank. We cleaned them out and filled them with gasoline. Rob found a large piece of metal to put on the wood floor of the deck that was placed under the small charcoal grill for cooking. We packed a cooler with food and drinks. Our sleeping bags were wrapped in plastic, along with our rain gear and Robbie's banjo.

I had been a Boy Scout, achieved swimming and lifesaving merit badges so I felt confident if a worst-case scenario happened. There were life jackets on board. He did not take a compass because we planned to follow the coastline to Leamington, Ontario.

Friday morning on a summer day we headed out from the MRYC. We left early and felt we could make it to Leamington in one day. We had perfect weather and a calm lake.

We were making about five miles an hour and decided to take a tack closer to a direct line to Leamington, which put us further from the coastline. We were navigating by sight since we had no navigation tools. It was a slow ride. We took turns steering and stayed clear of lake freighters. As the sun was going down, we spotted a small stone harbor and a building behind it. Turned out to be a VFW Post and we missed our mark. We were in Colchester, Ontario, twenty miles west of Leamington. It was almost dark. We thought it was strange because we saw very few small boats. An older couple had been watching us tie up the raft and came over and introduced themselves. They had never seen a pontoon raft. That part of the lake was not well suited for small boats due to rough weather. They invited us into their club for the Friday night fish fry. We had a delicious fish supper and my first beer, a Carling Black Label, 12 percent. Whew! In USA it was 7 percent. It did not bother me though. As more members figured out who we were and what we showed up in we were celebrities, and they bought our supper.

We spent the night sleeping on the raft deck. In the morning after breakfast at the VFW, we left for Leamington, Ontario. We made it to our destination in suitable time. There were no docks, so we beached the raft. A few curious people came over to see this strange craft. Rob asked for directions to the mayor's hardware store.

Robby had written several weeks before we left and told the mayor about our trip. The mayor seemed surprised that we came. He called the local newspaper and they met us at the raft and took our photo. We were on the front page of the *Leamington Star*. Wow! Sixteen years old and we were rock stars.

The mayor gave us permission to camp on the beach for the five days we stayed. The townspeople came to meet and greet us. They also had never seen a pontoon raft and told us how brave we were for taking this trip in these dangerous waters.

One day a group of divers our age showed up with their gear and spear guns and said if we took them out to the reef, they would catch our supper. So, we did. That evening we grilled fish. They brought sweet corn and all their friends. About twenty-five people show up. Several brought guitars since the newspaper said Rob was a folk singer and brought his banjo. We had a bonfire, good food and folk music. We sang the popular folk songs of the day: Peter Paul and Mary, Bob Dylan, Joan Baez, and The New Christie Minstrels. That evening was the highlight of our trip. I will never forget it.

The morning we left, the lake was calm, but it was foggy. We decided to throw caution to the wind and head out on a straight line to Toledo by sight. LOL, we could not see anything through the fog. It was a less than perfect day, with no visibility and small waves on the lake. The further out we were away from land we became apprehensive about our decision to not to follow the coast. We could see nothing but water 360 degrees. We tried to stay straight. The only boats we saw were lake freighters. Early afternoon after the fog lifted, we spotted land in the far distance and a boat coming our way. As it came closer it looked like a patrol boat. OMG it was the Coast Guard! Seems like we were in the Camp Perry firing range. Holy Toledo! Thank the dear Lord they were not shooting that day. After they read us the riot act, we were escorted out of harm's way. We made it back to the Maumee River Yacht Club by night fall. It was a great adventure for me, the first of many.

Rob went on to open a beatnik coffee shop on Monroe Street in Toledo named "Like Mother's" where folk singers would congregate. You had to be 18 to get in. Even though I was underage I always had a free pass. He eventually moved to San Francisco.

CHAPTER 8

My Introduction to the FBI

Since today is my 73rd birthday, my mother's famous words always ring true on this day: "At the rate you're going you'll never make it to 16!"

I was not the perfect little boy. I got into my share of trouble. I was not a bad boy; I just had a mischievous side ... occasionally.

I was about 13 or 14 when the principal at St. James called me to her office. There I met an FBI agent. Holy Toledo ... I was in the bad box! About a week earlier, my best friend Tom Erdman, who lived down my block, and I were playing softball in the street with John Welter. His house was in the 600 block of Brighten Street two blocks away from my home. Unintentionally my ball went into John's neighbor's yard across the street. Mr. Hitchsky was a grouchy old man and gave us a tough time about playing ball in the street and occasionally it rolled in his yard. Several times on that day our ball ran into his yard. We would run over and retrieve it. We did not hurt his yard. Then it happened. He came off the porch and took our ball and would not give it back. Just like that. We could not believe it. He took our ball and went into the house. We were pissed!

My older brother Jim had some silver salute firecrackers in his stash. A silver salute was more powerful than a cherry bomb. Tom Erdman and I fashioned a longer wick with a melted crayon and string. We had a plan.

For Sunday morning Toledo *Blade* delivery, I slept on the couch in the living room because I had to get up at 4:30 in the morning. The Sunday papers were delivered in two sections that had to be assembled and delivered in a wagon before 6 a.m. It took a lot of time. That morning I woke up about 2 a.m. and quietly went out the front door and walked down the street to Tom's house. He tied a piece of fishing string around his wrist and dropped the weighted end out his second-story bedroom window. I snuck between his and his neighbor's house and gave a yank on the string. Two minutes later he snuck out the front door. We quietly walked in the shadows past Mahala King's house, down Grafton Street two short blocks and made our way to the grouch's house across from John Welter's.

We already attached the extra-long wick to the salute several days before. We put the silver salute in Hitchsky's mailbox that was mounted on the side of his house next to his side door, lit the wick with a match and took off running like a cat chasing a mouse. We got to the corner of Grafton and Nicholas Street when it exploded! KABOOM! We looked at each other and said, "The wick wasn't long enough!" The plan had been to be back home in bed before it went off. We tried to keep our gut-splitting laughs on the quiet side. Just like you are now. We made it home quietly and back to bed like nothing happened.

A couple of days later I was being interview by the FBI in the principal's office. It seems that blowing up a mailbox was a federal offense. I did not lie about it and agreed to pay the cost of a new mailbox and the glass that was blown out of the side storm door next to the mailbox. (I am splitting a gut writing this.) Lesson learned ... a small cherry bomb would have achieved the desired result and done much less damage.

Do not go away, folks, there is more to the story. When the weather was warm, I rode my bike to school, so I could go right to the paper station and deliver my papers. I was about three doors away from my house when big brother Jim intercepted me. "Don't go home," he said. "The FBI was out and talked to Mom. You're in big trouble!" *Mmmm* what to do? I made the decision to run away. I knew the drill sergeant would take me to the woodshed for a meeting with Mr. Belt. We feared our father. I asked Jim to go home and get my suede jacket and my bank book (I had $20). Jim had my back. After he brought my coat and bank book, I high tailed down to Tom's, and he decided to run away with me.

We took off on our bikes and hid out under a bridge at the state asylum about a mile away. The asylum was on several hundred acres at Detroit and Arlington Streets. We felt safe there. Big brother brought us burgers and cokes for several days and delivered my papers for me. He did not rat us out. After several days and nights, we gave it up and went home. It was not easy for me to admit defeat. Fortunately for me my father only grounded me for a month. I could only leave for school, church and to deliver my papers. I was caught twice sneaking out and had two more weeks tacked on. Sooo, six weeks was not easy. Part of that was during summer vacation.

Adversity brings opportunity.

I spent my time building and customizing model cars in my makeshift studio in the basement. I practiced my pinstriping every day and pinstriped a few bikes.

My good friend John Welter died from Pancreatic cancer five years ago. Tom Erdman was a special friend. He was a hunk, blond hair, and blue eyes. He was a chick magnet.

He came down with MS at nineteen. He married, had a son, and his wife bought him a Corvette. He often stopped by my race shop on Tedrow Street in the south end. The last time I saw him alive, he was in a strapped in a wheelchair and could not speak. He soon passed away.

CHAPTER 9

The Evils of Alcohol

My first job as a sign painter was at Wally Sign Company when I was 15 years old. I started out as the shop boy sweeping floors and general cleanup for $1.10 an hour. I learned the art of layout, color, hand lettering, silk-screening, gold-leaf lettering, billboards, and walls. There were four of us. I soon learned hard lessons about people and their struggles in life. For Wally, the owner, it was collecting his accounts receivables and managing two employees who were alcoholics. My parents were not drinkers, maybe a drink at the holidays. There was never beer or wine in our home. Wally Wozniak. and Bob Harder were good, industrious men. Both men struggled to come to work on Monday mornings after drinking all weekend. Wally Wozniak, I grew particularly fond of. He was a sweet, kind man who had fallen on tough times because of his addiction. He had a degree in engineering and after 20 years lost his job at Teledyne, the engine manufacturer of the Tomahawk Missile on Laskey Road because of his drinking. He lost his wife, children, home, and car. He lived in a rooming house above the Peacock bar a block away on Monroe Street and walked to work. There were four rented rooms and a shared bathroom. Wally Wozniak was at the bottom of the barrel.

One Monday when he did not show up for work, I walked two doors away to George's Restaurant on the corner at lunch time and picked up a carry out chicken noodle soup and a black coffee. I walked another block away to the Peacock bar, went upstairs and knocked on Wally's door. He struggled to get out of bed. I felt so bad for this man. He was very appreciative for the soup and coffee. When I returned to the shop Wally the owner asked where I had been. He then proceeded to tell me not to be an enabler. "Alcoholics will never recover until they decide to quit drinking." I made the decision that day to not drink. On a rare occasion I may have a beer or liqueur after a healthy meal.

In later years, my good friend, the infamous civil rights attorney C. Thomas McCarter invited me to a dinner with his hard-drinking union clients. After dinner, I ordered a grasshopper. LOL Tom about split a gut and still reminds me to this day how his bad ass biker friend Michael embarrassed him in front of his clients.

When you are the low man on the totem pole, you are the gofer: Go for this and go for that! I daily made a run for a Wally Delvaux coffee, blond and sweet. I never drank coffee until I went to work at Wally's. I still drink mine blond and sweet.

A year into my apprenticeship, I was doing rather decent work. My side hustle painting names and pinstriping on hot rods was doing well. I went to my first car show "Autorama" at the Civic Auditorium on Erie Street about 1960. I had my sign kit and dressed the part of a beatnik artist, black turtleneck, black pegged pants, black boots, and a black beret. (You need to have a little showmanship.) There I met Warren Bookman, the promoter and Bernie Solomon his sidekick. Good men and now lifelong friends. Warren gave me a weekend pass to my first show and many thereafter. Now I needed to find my first job at the show. I went up to a car owner who had built a beautiful hot rod that had a plain Jane paint job and no one looking at his car. I was new to the trade, so I had to use my salesmanship. I told him I did the first job free and guaranteed him I could draw a crowd to look at his cool car and someday I would be famous. That did the trick. I would put on a show for the crowd. My expertise was pinstriping long thin lines down the side chrome molding and cool designs on the nose, over the headlights and on the deck lid, then the car name. After stirring and mixing the paint I would sprinkle baby powder on my hands, palette my brush to just the right consistency and proceed to paint a four-foot-long stripe next to the chrome molding without lifting the brush. I would tell the crowd to hold their breath as I was holding mine. My captive audience was spellbound. "How can that little brush hold so much paint?" "Wow! Look how straight that is!" "He sure has a steady hand." "I watched a sign painter once who had the shakes so bad until he went to his sign kit, pulled out a pint of whiskey, took a slug and his shakes went away."

I went from one car to another to another. All weekend. I charged $5 a side for a car name in two colors and $25–$30 to stripe the car. Some of the car names were (Renegade, Apache, Villain, Rambunctious, Baby Bonneville, E Plurbis Unum, Follow Me, Digger, Mohammed).

I tagged along with new older friends to cars shows during the winter. The show promoters paid mileage and hotel for the entrants to travel from outside the area. All I had to do was buy my meals.

Same outfit, same routine ... I painted the first car free, and the flood gates would open: Detroit, Cleveland, Lima, Cincinnati, Indianapolis, etc. I was making $200–$300 hundred dollars a weekend.

I lived on cheeseburgers and vanilla milkshakes.

I made many friends amongst the hot-rodders. A few guys were very instrumental in my success because they referred me to anyone they encountered. The Roberts Twins, Gary, and Terry lived four blocks away on Colton Street A mere three minutes away on my bike. I painted on so many cars I cannot begin to count in their garages and driveways. They never asked for a dime for all the work they sent me. They built some of the coolest cars in Toledo. Their work could compete with the California custom builders. Another good friend was Robie. He went to Macomber High and if I was standing at the bus stop on Spencer Street, he would pick me up and drop me off at Central High Catholic High School. He referred me a great deal of work. Terry Shuman also spread the word and was a lifelong friend. He died several months ago.

Terry Roberts died several years ago. Good man, old friend. I will never forget he and Gary's kindness. My dear friend Robie passed away last winter.

CHAPTER 10

Got Caught Smoking at School

My first year at Central Catholic High School was most exciting. I went to a Catholic grade school; mass was every day, five days a week and on Sunday. I was also an altar boy.

Central had a three-day retreat. Mass every day, lecture after lecture, by the third day I was getting bored. I went to another lecture after lunch and decided I needed a smoke. I stepped outside by Mettler Street; it was in the dead of winter and was snowing. I was hiding around the corner of the school building when a nun came out and saw me. I had just taken a long drag on a Kent cigarette. "Follow me," said the good nun. I had just been busted. The price you paid if you were caught smoking on school grounds was eight (demerits) penalty halls at 45 minutes each after school. UGH!

I went back into building and followed the nun until she passed the corner of the "L" shaped wing on the north side of the building. She went straight, I took a left turn and ran down the hallway, down the steps around the corner, down another flight to the basement slipped and fell because my shoes were wet from standing in the snow outside. I only fell two steps but stuck my hand out to break my fall. *Snap!* I broke my left wrist. The only classroom in the basement was the art class, which I knew would be locked. Before the art room was a door to the school's boiler room. I tried the doorknob, and it was open. I went inside and hid behind the huge boilers. Five minutes passed, then ten. After about 15 minutes I evaded the long arm of the law.

I opened the door a crack and saw no one. I snuck down the hall and slowly went up the steps to the hallway. Not a soul was in sight. I had a ready excuse in case I was stopped. One could go to confession at any time during the retreat. I was prepared. My wrist was throbbing in pain.

When I got to the corner of the two halls, I peeked around the corner and the coast was clear. The last session of the day was a guest speaker in the gym on the first floor. The doors were closed, and they were heavy. So much for quietly sneaking in.

The gym was packed. Our principal, Monsignor Harrington, was sitting on the end of the bleachers and pointed to a seat next to him. Oh no! I took a seat and did not realize I smelled of smoke.

My left wrist swelled up and was really hurting. I started to cry the pain was so great. He asked what was wrong, so I showed him the broken wrist. He took me to his office and called my mother. She had no car and Dad was working. He drove me to St. Vincent's hospital a few blocks down the street.

We went into the emergency room. I walked out two hours later with a cast on my wrist and my arm in a sling.

He drove me home and now I had to face my parents. No way was I going to tell the whole story.

I graciously thanked the good monsignor for his kindness. I did not feel I deserved it. He smiled ☺.

I thought everything was cool until I got to school Monday morning. There was a note on my locker to go to the school office. *Mmm!* I walked into the office and was handed a demerit slip. Eight big ones.

CHAPTER 11

Egg Toss in the Hallway

My first year at Central Catholic High School, I had a class right after lunch on the first floor near the Mettler Street entrance right next to the Sister Gregory's bookstore. While waiting for class to start, Jim Himes tossed me a hard-boiled egg. The hall was filled with students. I tossed it back. Jim moved about 10 feet back and tossed it again. I caught it and moved about 15 feet back. He then wound up and threw it at me hard. I caught it and wound up and threw it with everything I had! It ricocheted off the ceiling and exploded "KABOOM" on the bookstore counter all over Sister Gregory, several students close by and the only African American female student in the school! I never knew an egg could break into so many pieces. OMG! It was an accident, but how do you convince the "Gestapo" of that.

We took the only option! Run like hell! Jim took off one way and I the other. Holy Toledo, what just happened? I could not believe it. I ran down the hall, turned the corner and ran up all three flights of stairs to the third floor and hid in the men's room.

The bell rang which meant you had five minutes to be in your classroom. I walked nonchalantly down the steps and headed for my classroom as if nothing happened. My heart was pounding as I got closer to my classroom. There was a crowd in front of the bookstore, including Father Waltz (assistant principal and disciplinarian), Monsignor Harington and several other teachers. I was scared. I walked into the room, spotted Himes, and looked away. He looked as scared as me except I was the one that threw the egg. I was in deep shit if anyone ratted me out.

The bell rang just as we got into our seats. Luckily, I had a seat in the back. I could hide behind the person in front of me. Jim was closer to the front of the class-room. The teacher, Father Waltz and Monsignor Harrington were in and out of the classroom for about 10 minutes talking in hushed tones. They never looked at Himes or me. Finally, the teacher walked back in the classroom and shut the door and started class. Whew! I had dodged a bullet and used one of my nine lives.

My mother's prediction was coming into fruition, "At the rate you're going, you're not going to make it to 16."

CHAPTER 12

Smoke Bomb in the Bathroom

My oldest sister, Ann Schings, was dating a sailor after she graduated from Central Catholic High School. He was over one day and gave me a military grade smoke bomb. It was about the size of four silver salutes. What does a 16-year-old, all-American kid do with a smoke bomb? Light, it up, of course!

I took it to school the next day. It was so cool I had to do something special with it. *Mmmm* the lightbulb went off. The boy's restroom at Central had urinals on the left side and stalls on the right. The regular stall doors were open about two feet above the floor. The faculty had a stall where the door was only six inches of open space above the floor and required a key to open.

I asked my two best friends, Gordon Capshaw and Jim Nicholson, to be the lookouts for me. The perfect time was right after lunch. I waited until no one was in the restroom. There was a set of steps leading to the outside next to the first-floor john. I ran outside and lit a cigarette, tore the filter off and cupped the cigarette in my hand and hurried back inside. The boys nodded that the coast was clear. I went inside and put the cigarette over the wick and left about a half an inch from the flame to the top of the wick, so I would have time to get away before the wick lit the smoke bomb. I rolled the smoke bomb under the door in the faculty stall and walked out. It was hard to not split a gut.

My homies and I walked down the hall about 50 feet and pretended to carry on a conversation while keeping an eye on the door. It seemed like an eternity before someone came along and opened the door. Along came a kid who opened the door. OMG the smoke poured out along with the smell of sulfur. There was smoke everywhere. He ran across the hall to the school office to report it. Along came another kid who opened the door. More smoke! The smoke-filled hall was filling up with students changing classes. Suddenly, someone set the fire alarm off! It was not me. I had not planned on this. Holy Toledo. Fire alarms were going off throughout the school! We had all practiced fire drills. Even with the restroom door closed smoke poured out at the bottom of the door. I did some research on smoke bombs. Small bombs like the one I had could put out 40,000 cubic feet of smoke. Can you imagine a military grade one going off? OMG!

No one panicked, but everyone was getting out of the building fast. Central has four entry/exit doors. Students and faculty were going outside from every direction—2,100 students and 100 faculty members rushing outside. My heart was racing; I could be in deep shit! If I was caught, this was no eight demerits this was suspension or expulsion!

Do you know what happens when a fire alarm goes off in a school? The alarm goes straight to the fire department. Sirens were coming from every direction. Jesus Jenny!

Dear Lord! I was not planning on this. I hope I do not get caught! I was saying my prayers in one breath and laughing my ass off with the next! This was BIG! I was digging deep asking the Lord's help. I counted how many prayers I said in my many years of going to church and as an altar boy. I hoped my prayer reserve was enough to cover this desperate plea for help.

OMG! More fire engines.

Everyone was milling around outside. It was easy for me to get lost in the crowd. My bros and I played it cool. No time for bragging rights.

Mum was the word. The smoke was cleared, and we went back inside. After several days and not being summoned to the principal's office, I concluded that my prayers were answered.

I got away with that one and made a vow to never pick up a smoke bomb again. By the time I graduated from Central, I figured I used about half of my nine lives and my prayer reserve was depleted.

CHAPTER 13

Painting Billboards

I had many memorable fun times working with Wally. My favorite day was a warm summer day when we lettered a billboard or wall outside. T-shirt, shorts, and boots. We preferred to start early in the morning with a goal of lettering the billboard in one day.

One time we had a 10 by 40-foot billboard to letter in the Colony, a triangular corner at Central and Monroe Streets in Toledo. We used 12-foot "A" ladders that extended to 20 feet and a 20-foot aluminum plank. We had sun all day. Several days earlier the shop crew primed and finish-coated the raw plywood. Wally made a small-scale drawing then proceeded to draw the large letters with charcoal sticks and a yardstick. He was a pro. I followed behind and painted the letters.

We were in the sun most of the day with heat bearing down. It got to the point where it was miserably hot! Wally took a break and walked over to a carry out and bought quarts of orange juice and lemonade. If you ever want to know what rotten eggs taste like, drink orange juice and then a cup of lemonade. OMG it was horrible! We had a good laugh and never did that again. I learned a lot from Wally in many ways.

Ten years later when I was on my own, I had three billboards 10 by 30 feet to paint and letter at the Lucas County Rec Center in Maumee, Ohio. It was just before baseball season in the cool month of April. Hertz, Avis, and Holiday Inn billboards were about to come to life. I challenged myself to paint and letter all three in one day. I took a helper with me, and we started at dawn. First, we undercoated all three billboards with Sherwin-Williams fast dry primer. Next, we rolled on the backgrounds, yellow for Hertz, red for Avis and green for Holiday Inn with fast dry finish enamel. I drew the large letters with white chalk sticks, from a scale drawing I made of the Hertz sign. Easy, five black letters on the yellow background. I painted the outline of the letters, and my helper filled them in. It was not as easy as it sounds. Moving the ladders and plank took time. Next the Avis sign with white letters on a red background. The Holiday Inn billboard was last and took much longer because it had a special logo plus the lettering-in script.

We finished in the dark with the headlights from my truck. In sixteen hours, we had completed the job. After expenses I made about $2,500. That was big money in 1970 for a good day's work. It is always very satisfying to go back later and admire your work.

I graduated from Central Catholic High in 1962 and Wally gave me my Journeyman's Sign Painter's card. I also improved my grades to four As and two Bs. I was a four-year art major which was a double period. I had straight As for all four years in art. I never liked English and here I am authoring a book!

CHAPTER 14

Hot Rod Harry

In the summer of 1962, I bought my first car, a 1958 Chevrolet Impala Convertible: 348cid engine, four-barrel carburetor, a stick shift with three on the tree (column) for 700 dollars. One of my haunts was Al and Chuck's Sohio at South and Spencer Streets. Al Baker and Chuck Knott were my customers years earlier on my paper route on Nicholas Street, so I knew them. They had a '40 Ford pickup truck, maroon with an Oldsmobile engine with three two-barrel carburetors. "The Hauler" was parked at the station. I rode my bike up there often as a kid just to admire it. They drag raced it on the weekends. Yes, I did a little work on my Chevy ... my friend Bob Haube, who later become my crew chief on The Murray Racing Team had two large brass bombshells as in Howitzer size, World War 2 vintage. He welded them to my exhaust system behind the front wheels. He made cutouts with plumbing pipe and caps. I could reach inside the bombshells, unscrew the caps, and have straight exhaust reverberating through the brass shells. No mufflers! The Chevy made big noise and sounded like a race car. One day I took it out to Vettes Ville Dragway at what is now known as Metcalf Field for my first drag race. I learned how to get a quick start from a standing start. This experience would come into play several years later when I started sports car racing. Hot Rod Harry was the proprietor. I pinstriped a few cars for Harry in the past.

He was one of Toledo's characters. Greasy looking, owned a body shop that fixed wrecked Cadillacs for a living. He had a side hustle as a preacher. One time he asked me to be the starter at his drag strip. This was before the Christmas tree lights become popular for starting the drag race. A drag race was a quarter mile long. Cars started from a dead stop. Whoever reached the end of the quarter mile first won. I had a red flag in one hand and the green flag in the other. It was very scary. The starter stood about 25 feet in front of both cars. I pointed the green flag at each driver to see if they were ready. They would nod their heads, and I dropped the green flag, and they would take off and fly by me, one car on either side.

This was exciting until a new guy showed up. Sneaky Pete Robinson raced a front engine slingshot dragster. He had a better idea. He drove his car to the start line. He then pulled a lever that jacked the rear tires off the ground about an inch. He stood on the gas, and the rear wheels were spinning. He dropped his wheels on the pavement and took off as I dropped the green flag. He pulled an incredible hole shot on his competitor. Scared the daylights out of me! That is when I retired from my starter's job.

CHAPTER 15

I Wrecked My Brother's Car "Rambunctious"

My older brother Jim is the brother you would always want to have. He was cool, got good grades, was an outstanding baseball pitcher in high school, college (University of Toledo). He was a successful businessman. As kids, he was kind and looked out for his siblings.

I was sixteen; he was seventeen and had purchased his first car, a 1955 Ford Fairlane black coupe with a 312cid V8 engine. He chose the name for his car, and I hand lettered it on the front fenders, white lettering with a red shadow. "Rambunctious" was a rock and roll instrumental by Duane Eddy.

One day he let me borrow his car. I picked my younger neighbor Bobby Schultz, who lived four doors away. I do not know what possessed me to do this ... I drove down the Anthony Wayne Trail to the edge of downtown Toledo on Collingwood at Erie Street, turned the car around and told Bobby, "Watch this. I'm going to go flat out through the sweeping curve from Collingwood to the Anthony Wayne Trail!"

I got on the gas, shifted through the three gears, and turned left in the three lanes of the Anthony Wayne Trail. (I was young and dumb with a minimal amount of experience.) I was halfway through the turn when the car started sliding sideways and then I lost control. I was inexperienced and did not let off the gas. The car jumped the curb in the median, shot across the incoming three lanes (fortunately there were no cars in my way) jumped another curb and went up the hill and came to a sudden stop when I hit a concrete abutment. This was before seat belts. Smoke came pouring out from a broken radiator and a fire started under the popped-up hood from an electrical short. The glove box popped open and out came bro's gross of silver salutes all over the floor.

Bobby and I slowly scrambled out of the burning car. I knew I was in deep trouble and had to think fast, I knew the police and fire department would arrive soon. I went over to the passenger side and helped Bobbie scoop up the silver salutes, the last thing I needed was an explosion. We threw them in the tall grass about 20 yards away. Handful after handful, we went back and forth. There were some kids that were playing on the hill above the concrete abutment and saw us throw the firecrackers in the weeds. They came down and quickly picked them up. That was fine with me.

I could hear the sirens and was shell shocked! The police and fire departments arrived. The fire was extinguished quickly. The police officer came over, asked for my license, and asked what happened. Thinking quickly, I knew I needed a good story, so I told him a dog ran out in front of me, I swerved and lost control. He bought it! Whew! Thank you, Jesus!

Somewhere in the aftermath I felt blood running down my right leg. My knee had smashed the key in the ignition switch and bent it completely in half. Bobby had a sore back but was otherwise okay. An ambulance took me to Mercy Hospital where they stitched me up. Nothing was broken. My mother had been called and she sent my uncle Joe Fournier to take care of me and bring me home. Dad was still working, and she had little ones at home. When I thought about how I was going to deal my strict father I had a panic attack in the ER. Several hours later, Uncle Joe took me home to face the music, my father. Mom must have said something to Dad because other than asking how it happened, he was not to upset. My fabricated tale worked once, why not try it again. Wait for it there is more ...

My accident made the next day's Toledo *Blade* newspaper. One year earlier, there was a huge accident on the Anthony Wayne Trail about a hundred yards from mine. A gasoline truck exploded, and two firefighters were killed. The writer tied my accident in with the memory of the previous year's horrific explosion.

It took all my savings ($550) to replace Jim's car. This time he bought a Ford convertible. I am not proud of this event in my past, but hey it happened. Life goes on.

I Moved Away from Home

Late 1962, Wally merged his business with the Toledo Sign Company on Huron Street. I was the only one that Wally took with him. Toledo Sign was one of Toledo's oldest sign companies. Orvld Heil, an older German with a ninth-grade education, had built a particularly good business over the years. There were eight employees plus Wally and me. Orv's reputation was second to none. He was honest to a fault. If he bid a job and it came in under his quote, he would give the customer a refund, if his expenses went over his estimate, he would complain about it to anyone who would listen and eat the loss.

There was only one problem for me there, His 21-year-old son was learning to hand letter, so I had to take a backseat to him. I understood and only stayed a year.

I tried college for a semester at the university in the college of business in 1963 but it did not fit for me. I saw too much drinking and cheating amongst my friends. I wanted to be a sign painter. Art was my true passion. The university had a minimal art program at the art museum so that was not an option.

I moved on to the Colonial Sign Company on Laskey Road across the street from the very first McDonald's in Toledo. Ken Pool and Dick Warnke had only been in business for a couple of years. Neither one was a sign painter. Jack Kriedel was the full-time sign painter. Their business was growing. It was a good opportunity. Ken was a full-time salesman and Dick ran the shop. Good men to work with.

Kenny and I got along so well that he asked me to babysit for his six children one night a week. Ken and his wife, Susie, were warm and kind loving parents. The children brought immense joy to my heart and many special memories. I will share several with you.

I moved away from home at age nineteen and I moved in with the Pool family on Sunnyside Drive in West Toledo, Marty was seven, Michael, six, Mary, five, Kathy, four, Susie, three, Karen, two and Molly, one. After I moved out, they had two more, Kenny and Patrick. Little Mary followed me everywhere; she liked the attention I gave her.

There was a full bath and two bedrooms that Ken built in the basement. Periodically Kathy and Susie (Susan Pool Brangman) would come downstairs in the morning and watch me shave. "Mikey Murray, he are putting his mask on," Kathy would say. I can still picture little Susie with her thumb in her mouth and her blankie over her shoulder.

One time Marty's mother overheard him saying some "bad" words. She marched him to the bathroom to introduce him to Mr. Soap. Marty would not open his mouth. He just clinched his teeth. Susie ran the soap over his teeth. He learned a lesson and received a nickname from me. He was now "Soapy."

After church one Sunday, I took the children to Betsy Ross Pancake House for breakfast on Monroe at Secor Road; they behaved like angels, were well-mannered and polite. I was 20 years old at the time. Towards the end of the meal an elderly couple walked over and complimented me on "my" well-behaved children and gave them each a nickel. I did not have the heart to tell them that I was just the babysitter.

The Pool family lived on Sunnyside Drive near Bennett Road in West Toledo, two doors away from Sunnyside Pool. I had good times swimming and playing with these sweet, precious children. They were a joy to be with. I drove a 1957 Austin-Healey roadster at the time and often took the kids for rides around the block with the top down.

Ken Senior, Michael, and Kathy have passed away.

CHAPTER 17

My Sports Car Addiction Begins

While still living with the Pools one of my best friends in high school, Gordon Capshaw, and I took a trip to Daytona Beach, Florida for spring break in 1964. Gordy was in the Sigma Phi Epsilon fraternity at the University of Toledo. His fraternity brothers were congregating at a motel on the beach. We drove my '57 silver Austin-Healey Roadster with blue competition stripes.

We were going to drive straight through from Toledo. There were no interstate highways at the time. There were two lane roads all the way. It started raining in Tennessee. It was not safe driving in the rain in the Healey. It had side curtains and the defroster left a lot to be desired. Visibility was poor. Somewhere along the way I saw a sign that said welcome to North Carolina. WHAT? I had taken a wrong turn somewhere and we were lost. North Carolina was about 200 miles east of where we needed to be. It was about 10 or 11 p.m. We stopped at a roadside cafe (combo gas, carryout, restaurant) and bought a Coke. Gordy and I were sitting on a step looking at a map when a big yellow 1955 Buick pulled up with gold sheriff's five point star on the door. Out came a big burly sheriff's deputy who looked like Buford T. Justice, the character played by Jackie Gleason in the movie "Smokey and the Bandit." "What y'all boys doing here?" "We are lost, officer," I said. After Buford checked my driver's license, he escorted us out of town and back to the highway pointed in the right direction.

It was a miserable trip in the rain. The Austin-Healey had side curtains with a large gap between the top of the side curtain and the top. It leaked like a sieve. Our feet were sloshing in the wet carpet on the floor. We constantly had to wipe the inside of the wet, fogged-up windshield.

We made it to Daytona Beach, Florida and found the motel and the frat boys. Half of them were drunk; empty beer cans were everywhere in the suite of rooms. In one room lying on the bed was Mike Ryan, a friend from Central Catholic. He was a fair-haired redhead and was beet red and covered in oil. He had spent too much time in the Florida sun. He lay there shaking. The brothers ended up taking him to a hospital.

One night while driving along the highway next to the Atlantic Ocean, we noticed many cars with their headlights on pointing into the ocean. We pulled on to the beach and saw a car in the ocean with waves rolling over the fenders. A group of kids were trying to push it back to shore. It was a lost cause. That same evening someone tried to jump in the pool from the second-floor balcony at our motel and missed.

He landed on the concrete apron around the pool. It was a bloody mess. He was taken to the hospital.

I was totally turned off by the college frat scene. I did not fit in with this group.

On the trip home we experienced a dead battery in the Healey. After we paid cash for a new battery, we had spent our gas money for getting home. Gordy's father had given him a Gulf credit card for emergencies. This was an emergency! We stopped frequently to top off the gas tank because there were few Gulf stations on the way home, and it was Easter Sunday weekend. Remember we were on a two-lane road. We asked the Gulf attendant to add a couple of bucks to the credit card as a tire repair. We bought a six pack of Coke, a loaf of white bread, a jar of peanut butter, grabbed an ice cream wooden flat spoon to spread the gooey peanut butter. That is all we ate until we got to Dayton.

Being good Catholic boys, we stopped in Dayton, Ohio, for Easter Sunday mass. We found a church; however, we had an hour to kill before the service. About a block away was an open bar with a neon sign that said, "Best burgers in town." We each had a burger and a cold beer with the extra cash we picked up from many "tire repairs." It was our first warm meal in two days. I figured I had earned a cold one.

By the time we made it to church the pews were well filled up. In a Catholic church the rear pews fill up first. Everyone was wearing his or her new Easter outfits. As we made our way to the front of the church, I noticed people staring at us. We were a sight. We had been up all night. My white Levi's were not very white anymore; neither was my once off-white kangaroo pullover jacket; we were unshaven and smelled of beer and onions.

We arrived home to eight inches that Easter Sunday in Toledo, Ohio. Not fun in a low hanging sports car.

Monday morning, Ken, Dick, and I met at 7 a.m. for breakfast at Frisch's Big Boy on Laskey Road just east of Tremainsville Road, and down the street from the sign shop. I decided to prank the boys that morning. I arrived a few minutes early, so I could grab a seat by the window. I wore the same clothes as the day before. I was grubby and unshaven for effect. They took a second look when they saw me; they sat down and quizzed me about my vacation. As I my telling my stories, I picked up the water cup and poured the water into cold air vent next to the seat about a foot above the table next to the window. They had a blank look on their faces as if to say, what is he doing? I proceeded to unzip the chest pocket on my kangaroo pullover and pulled out a beer, broke the tab and poured the cold beer into the water glass. I told them I had come of age.

CHAPTER 18

"California or Bust 1965"

Shortly after my October birthday, my girlfriend, Karen, and I broke up for good. For years I had been thinking about moving to California, hot rod heaven. There were cool cars in the Midwest but there were thousands more on the West Coast. I dreamed of pinstriping all of them. LOL. The gypsy in me said there is no better time to leave than now.

I sold my '57 Austin-Healey and bought a newer one. Charlie Koka owned a small import car dealership on Sylvania Avenue. I had been eyeing a 1962 Austin-Healey, vanilla white with red interior in the showroom window for a couple of weeks. I stopped and bought it. Packed my bags for a six-week exploratory trip. The clutch went out the night before I left. I drove it anyway and knew I would have to get a new one before I drove through the mountains. You can drive a car without a clutch with some expertise just by double clutching between shifts.

I headed out on old Route 66, a two-lane road, and drove to Denver, Colorado. I stopped at Kumpf Motor Sales in Denver to get my clutch replaced. They sold Ferrari, British Leyland, Rolls Royce, and Austin-Healey. The next day I was on my way. I was in awe driving through the beautiful mountains. My destination was Pasadena, California. My Godmother and favorite aunt, Pat Griffin, my mother's baby sister, was expecting me. My goal was to explore the West Coast and find a job in a sign shop. During the first week I was at Aunt Pat and Uncle Terry's house, they did their best to entertain me. One rainy day, Aunt Pat wanted to take me to the Art Linkletter TV show, "The Price is Right." She won a dishwasher, her first. Sign painters were in demand there and I applied everywhere.

I then went to visit my Aunt Katie and Uncle Dick's home in Escondido near San Diego. Aunt Katie was my mother's oldest sister. She was Admiral Nimitz's secretary during World War 2 and married a navy man.

Uncle Dick was the controller at Hawthorn Machinery, the largest Caterpillar dealership on the west coast. As an aside, years later the owner of the dealership was kidnapped. Uncle Dick received the call to assemble the $500,000 cash to pay the ransom. His boss escaped before the payoff and the FBI caught the kidnapper. I loved

San Diego. While there, my cousin Steve See took me to a folk festival at San Diego State University. I saw the famous folk singer Elizabeth Cotton perform the song she wrote, "Freight Train." She was a small African American woman who was left-handed and played the guitar upside down. She was amazing!

I went back to Los Angeles and received a phone call from a gal I dated in high school. She heard I was in California and invited me to stay with her and her two roommates in San Francisco. I drove the famous Route 1 along the coast. The most beautiful drive I had ever been on. The top was down, and the scenery was a remarkable sight.

Lois Johnson, her younger sister, and another friend rented a two-bedroom flat at the corner of Sacramento and Hyde in the beatnik-hippy neighborhood of Haight-Ashbury in San Francisco. Each day, one of them took a day off work and showed me the sights. We rode the trolley everywhere. The Golden Gate Bridge, Sausalito, Lombard Street, and several folk music coffee houses just for starters. They were wonderful hosts. I found a job I was interested in at Joe Lippo Signs. I told him I would be back after I returned home to have a going away party and pack the rest of my belongings.

My last night in San Francisco, the girls and their friend Harvey, a merchant marine sailor, and I had dinner at the Franciscan Restaurant on Fisherman's Wharf. After dinner Harvey wanted to take me to the red-light district, the famous North Beach. The girls were under 21, so Harvey and I went alone. Oh my! We went to the Condor Club and saw the famous Carol Doda, who made topless Go-Go dancing a household word. I did not look though! LOL! For a sheltered Midwest boy, it was shock and awe! Holy Toledo! We were packed in like sardines and sat at a small round table. Drinks were $5 each (big money for those days) and you had to buy two. The lights went out, the music started, and the spotlight shone on a pink grand piano with white fur around the legs suspended from the ceiling. As the piano lowered, there was Carol Doda dancing topless. An evening I will never forget. Topless bars up and down the street, they even had topless shoeshine stands.

The next morning, I said goodbye to my friends and told them I would be back soon. I drove back to Pasadena and said goodbye to my sweet Aunt Pat.

On the return trip back to Toledo, I sang the song, "If you're going to San Francisco be sure to wear some flowers in your hair." It was being played constantly on my Austin-Healey's radio. I was a dreamer; I was making plans and dreaming big about my return to San Francisco.

CHAPTER 19

The Perma Bench Company

U pon my return from California, I sat down with my parents and told them about my plans to relocate to California. My dad said wait a minute, I know where there is a good opportunity for you here in Toledo. My father had started a new career as a debit salesman for the Prudential Life Insurance Company about 10 years earlier. He was never ambitious. He would collect his debit route in the morning and play cards at the Republican Club in the afternoon. He was a dyed-in-the-wool Democrat, former Teamster, and the treasurer of the life insurance salesman's union. He did not care what your political affiliation was when it came to playing cards. He made his sales calls in the evening.

He played cards with a man by the name of Carlton Klein, who owned the Perma Bench Company. An outdoor advertising bus bench company with 400 benches in the Toledo area. Mr. Klein wanted to retire and sell the business. My dad thought it was a perfect business for me. My father was not the type to encourage me. He tried to discourage me from becoming an artist because he said that I would starve. I proved him wrong and that I had a lot going for me. For the first time he was encouraging me.

The sales price was $20,000. I did not have that kind of money I was just 21 years old. I thought about it overnight and decided to pursue it. (Good opportunities rarely come along.)

The more I thought about it the more I felt that I was a good fit. I was a good salesman, a sign painter and had great passion for whatever I decided to do. We met with Mr. Klein; he explained how the business worked. It made sense to me. He was paying out a sizable percentage to a sign company to design and silk screen his bench ads. I could do this myself. It was a no-brainer. When I got home, I told my dad that there was only one way I could do it. I knew my father had only six months left to pay on his house, and it would be free and clear. His payment was $52 a month. I had $2,000 and if he would refinance our home for $8,000, I would make his last six house payments for him. I could then make a 50 percent down payment for the business. I asked Mr. Klein to carry a note for the other $10,000 that I would pay off in two years. My father and mother agreed; Mr. Klein agreed. I went to the bank with dad;

Ohio Citizens made the loan. I was in business and $18,000 in debt. A Dodge pickup came with the deal, so I sold my '62 Austin-Healey and had some operating capitol.

I was not moving to California.

I converted our two and a half car garages into a sign shop and made an adjustable drawing board and benches for silk screening. A rented storage and workshop on Prouty Street off Broadway near my former grade school St. James came with the business.

I was in business. I had an immediate income from about 60 percent of the benches rented. My customers were First Federal S & L, United Savings S & L, Lucas County State Bank, and many others. The rate they paid was $6–10 a month per location on one-year contracts. My mother did my billing and kept track of the finances; my brother Jim did my taxes. I hired my retired Uncle Art to repaint all the benches a medium gray. They had been neglected for a long time.

My new routine was put on a coat and tie and sell ad space in the morning, Levi's and design, layout, cut film for silk screens and print the signs in the afternoon and evening. Saturdays, I put up signs and changed out the old green backs and seats with freshly painted gray ones.

In no time I was almost 100 percent leased out. My first new customer was Jerry Parmalee at the Par Four restaurant on Ashland Avenue. I knew Jerry because I had been a substitute hat check boy for my friend Gordon Capshaw in high school. I also offered an exclusive sign painting service to my customers.

As an aside, Jerry Parmelee was murdered in a botched robbery attempt several years later. He was a good man and always paid on time.

I was making good money, paying off my debt early so it was time for a new 1966 British racing green Austin-Healey.

CHAPTER 20

My First 1966 Shelby GT350

B rondes Ford was a large advertiser in all the media at the time. I remember the TV ads with Don Brondes taking a sledgehammer, smashing the windshield, and saying, "Brondes Ford is smashing prices!" These ads were everywhere, TV, radio and in print.

I decided to make a pitch and try to sell them a lesser expensive form of advertising to complement their current ads. Bus bench advertising was out there 24/7, had high visibility on most major intersections and was less expensive.

My predecessor used a small wooden bench about eight inches long and had the sign company make a small full color ad that he taped to the small bench. I subscribe to the philosophy "Why be ordinary when you can be extraordinary?" Go BIG. I made a full-size ad 2 by 6 feet on show cardboard. The name "BRONDES FORD" appeared in fluorescent orange letters on a dark blue background. I scored the sign in two places on the back side, so I could fold it into thirds, and it was easier to carry.

I made a cold call on Phil Brondes, Sr. While waiting to see him. I was eyeing the beautiful 1966 Shelby GT350, blue with white competition stripes in the showroom next to the amazing maroon 1966 Shelby Cobra roadster. The Shelby GT350 was $3,700 and the Cobra roadster was $7,200. I was a racing fan and had been following both soon-to-be legends.

I introduced myself and opened my full-sized presentation sign. He smiled and said, "Sit down, son." He was very pleasant, so I made my sales pitch. He listened intently. He then proceeded to tell me. "Here at Brondes Ford our advertising philosophy is quite simple. **We strive for two dollars' worth of advertising for every dollar we spend; our ads stand out above the crowd.**" He then picked up an empty Coke bottle by the neck and said, "I ought to break this bottle over your head, so you never forget the lesson I taught you today." "Yes sir, Mr. Brondes, believe me I'll never forget you, this day, and the fine lesson you taught me!" I did not forget the lesson and we still live by it today at Pamela Rose Auction Co. LLC; our ads own the page. It was a profound lesson in advertising. He complimented me on my sign.

He noticed that I was staring at the beautiful blue Shelby GT350 when he came out from his office to meet me. He proposed that we trade bench advertising for the car. DEAL!

We signed the contracts, they put a 30-day tag on her, and I drove my Shelby home. I was in gearhead heaven. I was 22 years old and had two new sports cars: a '66 Austin-Healey and a '66 Shelby GT350.

My little brother Bill (13) was home when I drove up in the new Shelby and wanted to go for a ride. We drove Nicholas Street to Spencer, to South Street to the Anthony Wayne Trail. I turned right and headed towards the zoo and lit her up! He still remembers that ride.

CHAPTER 21

Obtaining My Racing License

When I bought my first sports car, a 1957 Austin-Healey, through friends, I heard that one could practice their driving skills on Tontogany Creek Road. It was off Route 65 and 582 between Perrysburg and Grand Rapids, Ohio. The road width was very narrow, winding with several blind turns. I only did this at night, so I could see headlights if someone was coming towards me. I made a quick pass and then got out of there in case someone called the sheriff. I did it with all three Austin-Healey's. I had the need for speed.

I joined the FIASCO (Fort Industry Auto Sports Car Club of Ohio) sports car club. A good, fun bunch of enthusiasts. They had monthly meetings at Frisch's on Haverhill south of Phillips Avenue. The group held a half a dozen solo time trials at Toledo Speedway or in large parking lots in the Westgate Area. Several members were turn marshals at Waterford Hills Road Racing course in Michigan and several were avid road rally participants. I even served one year as president. Today we have a FB group with many former members.

I really took to time trails starting with my '66 Healey. I put in a roll bar, widened the rims, and added big Goodyear Racing tires to the '66 Healey. I started winning my class and was feeling maybe I could be good at this. I sold the '66 Healey shortly after I bought the '66 Shelby GT350.

I was never an athlete; I played football and basketball in grade school and church basketball in high school. I was a second stringer. I needed to work and had no time for practice. I do believe that every child dreams of being a winner if they participate in sports. I was no exception. After putting a set of racing Goodyear's on the Shelby, I was not only winning my class, I frequently, won the fastest time of day trophy. I could turn better times than the big block Corvettes and the modified cars. The smart-ass Corvette owners would stop by my car, so they could listen to it rust. I showed them who the boss was. It was a good feeling. I was a winning athlete.

In 1967, my cousin Tom Escott, Jack Novak and I went to the Sebring, Florida,12-hour sports car endurance race and I saw Mario Andretti win the race in the yellow number 1 Ford GT40 MK IV. I will never forget it.

I was a big Ford fan. That race followed with a trip to the June Sprints at Elkhart Lake, Wisconsin, with Jack Novak and David Bobak. I was hooked.

One day, I hit a Cadillac in a parking garage in downtown Toledo and heavily damaged the front end. Rather than repair the sheet metal, I opted for a fiberglass tilt front end and a Phil Knight molded rear trunk lid with a spoiler. Chuck at Apex Auto Body on Cherry Street did the work. He was a good advertising customer and loved customizing cars. I silk screened "Cobra, Cobra, Cobra" a famous Shelby logo on the rear quarter panels then silver leafed the lettering.

The winter of '67, I prepared the Shelby for SCCA Racing in the Central division. Todd Hammitt was my ace mechanic and Bob Haube, owner of Nationwide Collision on Main Street in East Toledo, was my fabricator. My goal in 1968 was to obtain my SCCA national competition license. To do that I had to go to two approved racing schools (Waterford, Michigan, and IRP in Indianapolis, Indiana) I needed six hours of classroom and driving at speed on the course with an instructor at each school. The requirements also called for completing six regional races. I was successful at Waterford, Nelson Ledges, Mid-Ohio, Marlboro, Maryland, and IRP, Indiana. I needed one more race to obtain my national license and was it getting late in the year.

The December Christmas Classic in Green Valley, Texas was the last regional race in the whole US. I needed this race to complete the requirements. Todd could not get off work, so I asked my new friend Don Fritz if he wanted to go along and help drive our race car hauler. It was a 24-hour drive straight through one way. Haube, Don and I took the trip.

We made it to Green Valley, Texas. It was 60 degrees, we were in T shirts, and the Texans were in sheepskin coats warming their hands over a bonfire in a 55-gallon drum. It was hysterical! I was led to believe that Texans were tough. LOL.

For a race to count as one of the six required, you had to finish the entire race. I was not concerned about winning as much as I needed to finish. Mission accomplished in one year!

CHAPTER 22

Going Sports Car Racing

The Murray Racing Team at Indianapolis Raceway Park 1968

I moved my business to an office building on Secor Road and rented the back of the building with a four-car garage for a sign shop with space to keep the race car in and an office up front. Don's mother was my answering service when I was out. Don and I became friends for life. He became our engineer and expert fabricator.

I knew my 1966 Shelby GT350 would not be competitive in its class because of the fiberglass tilt front end and Weber carburetors so I traded it for '65 metal fastback. The team and I converted it to a GT350R clone. I bought the homologation papers and parts from Shelby American. Working evenings and weekends over the winter, we stripped the car of all unnecessary parts, seats, interior panels gutted the trunk, etc. Bob Haube moved the rear inner fenders in two inches and Mather Springs made us a new set of leaf springs that were an inch narrower. We also lowered the front upper control arms an inch as Shelby suggested. The purpose was to be able to use the wider Goodyear Trans-Am tires and wheels. We also added a Watt's link to the rear suspension.

We raced this car in the SCCA Central division in '68, '69', 70' and half of '71 with so-so results but had a lot of fun. Many third, fourth and fifth place finishes. Our main competitors were the 289cid Cobras that weighed 500 pounds less and the 327 Corvettes that had 38 more cubic inches than us. We considered it a victory to finish third. It was a steep learning curve. The National Champion, Alan Barker, was from our division. Alan won the national championship five years in a row. I have a delightful story about Alan I will share in a later chapter.

We raced on the weekends all over Ohio, Wisconsin, Illinois, Indiana, Maryland, and New Hampshire. I do have some good stories though.

We competed in the very first sports car race ever held at Michigan International Speedway. It was a national point race in 1968 and was a shakedown for the first professional race at MIS, a Trans-Am race two weeks later for the pony cars, Camaro, Mustang, Javelin, Barracudas, and Pontiac Trans-Am.

One of my heroes showed up, Jerry Titus, a former Shelby driver and a sedan Mustang national champion. He brought four new, never seen before Pontiac Trans-Am's. They were all white with blue competition stripes. I went over and introduced myself and shook his hand. I noticed his cars had no numbers, "Jerry where are your car numbers?" "Oh no, we left them at the shop." I told him his ship came in. I just happened to be a sign painter and would go back to Toledo, paint the numbers on round circles and return first thing in the morning. Don Fritz and I showed up the next morning and installed the numbers for him. He was very appreciative.

We were racing at Blackhawk Farms, in South Beloit, Illinois. We arrived Friday night, it was dark, and the track was not locked. The team was staying with my aunt and uncle nearby. I did not want to leave the car unattended, so I was asked for a volunteer to stay. No one raised their hand so the low man on the totem pole, "Gopher" Bob Mowery was selected. He asked that we bring him breakfast in the morning. No problem.

We arrived first thing Saturday morning and several people stopped me and were laughing, "What's so funny?" I said. Have you seen your Gopher? No. Everyone knew everyone amongst the racing teams. Gopher had blond hair, blue eyes, and a magnanimous personality. As we approached our rig, there was Gopher sitting on the hood of the race car hauler in a granny gown! Neck to toe in this flannel gown. Real men do not sleep in granny gowns. "Gopher, you're an embarrassment, get down off that hood and put your clothes on!"

Bob Mowery, aka "Gopher", showed up at our race shop at 2216 Tedrow in Toledo, Ohio, one day. He was 17, a high school senior, drove a red Mustang fast back and wanted to be a part of a racing team. He had no skills. We took a liking to him. He had no father and no siblings. We took him in and taught him about life and mechanics. We taught him personal hygiene, proper dress and how to polish his shoes. You know, the kinds of things big brothers do. We also found him his first date.

In 1969 we were racing at Elkhart Lake, Wisconsin. The engine broke in practice and I did not have a spare. We busted our butts all week and it was an eight-hour drive from Toledo. We were tired and disappointed. We loaded up and went back to the Siebkins Resort where we were staying. Don Fritz, whom I never had seen drink before, went to the bar and ordered a tall seven- seven. He laid a 10-dollar bill on the bar and got nine dollars and ten cents back. Then another and another. The last I heard he was lining up the dimes in a prefect row and was going to buy his last drink when he had nine dimes. I was long gone by then.

We raced on a shoestring. I could not afford to pay my team members; everyone paid their own way. I paid for the room and if eight people came we slept eight people in a room with two double beds.

The youngest slept on the floor. Don Fritz came to bed and was out fast. He woke up in the middle of the night to pee. He missed the bathroom door and opened the closet door and peed in Gopher's boots, the only shoes he brought with him.

CHAPTER 23

Time to Buy a Corvette

1968 Greenwood Corvette

In the summer of 1970, we were racing the Shelby GT350 at Mid-Ohio, near Mansfield. In the A/Production race a gold '68 Corvette Coupe came out of nowhere and blew the doors off the famous red and white Owens Corning Fiberglass Corvettes, which had been the national champions for several years. The Owens Corning cars had been dominating most every race, running one and two. Jerry Thompson and Tony Delorenzo were top-notch drivers and had a staunch support team and big bucks from Owens Corning Fiberglass.

John Greenwood went on to win the national championship named The American Road Race of Champions at Road America in Atlanta, Georgia, at the end of the season.

Little did I know then that I would own one of John's cars a year later. John and his brother Burt built a new Corvette for the Daytona 24-hour race in January 1971. John and Dickie Smothers (of the Smothers Brothers comedy team) won their class and seventh overall at the Sebring 12-hour in March. A remarkable achievement. I saw John at a race in May and asked if he would build the Murray Racing Team a new B Production Corvette with a small block Chevy engine. He said, "Let us do this, I'll sell you my current car and convert it to B/P for you. I have a new one I am building for

A/Production. You can have my car after the six-hour race at Watkins Glen in July. You and I will run as a team the balance of the year in A and B Production." We struck a deal on a handshake for $10,000. I had $5,000 and my mechanic, Todd Hammitt, loaned me the other $5,000. I sold my GT350 to Gopher and his friend Stan.

John was a gentleman to do business with. He did everything he said he was going to do. John won the six-hour race at Watkins Glen then set about rebuilding my race car with a small block B Production engine. He delivered it mid-August. We reeled off five consecutive second place finishes (Alan Barker was still the king) and our first win and track record at Brainerd to end the regular season.

We finished fourth in the points and were an alternate at the National Championships in Road Atlanta that October. There were six divisions across the country; the top three drivers were guaranteed to start the race. It did not look like any of the top three cars in our class were going to drop out, so I asked our friend Ike Knupp who was qualified in his Plymouth Barracuda, if he'd like to drive our car. He jumped at the chance. Ike qualified on the outside pole next to Alan Barker. In Sunday's warm-up before the race the engine blew a head gasket. We could not fix it in time, so we did not start the race.

In 1972, John signed a contract to race BF Goodrich radial street tires on the IMSA and FIA Circuits. I stayed with Goodyear, who supplied us with free tires for the season. There was a big Memorial Day race weekend coming up, with the feature race being a 500-mile race on Sunday. The B/P race was on Saturday. I asked Ike Knupp to be my co-driver.

I found a junk 427 cast big iron block engine at the Gulf station on the corner and paid $200 for it. Todd rebuilt it and we loaded it in the race truck. Our plan was to run the B/P race on Saturday and install the 427-big block that night for the UnCola 500 on Sunday. It was a 16-hour drive to Brainerd, Minnesota. We finished second on Saturday in the rain. That night I rented the tech barn for $3. LOL, it was a good thing we did because it rained all night. Many campers sought shelter from the rain in the barn. We had quite a crowd. Little engine was pulled no problem. The big engine went in no problem but fitting the new exhaust system was another story. Ike and I had to get some sleep, so we left the team to finish it up. We returned to the barn the next morning just as Todd was firing up the engine. The crowd cheered! It took the team all night to pull off the engine switch.

We started sixth (they used my B/P qualifying time). Our first professional race was about to start. We had never refueled or made a pit stop before. We were green. Ike was an incredible driver, so he started the race. It was a bright sunny day, so we did not have to worry about rain tires.

The race started and at the first pit stop it was like a Chinese fire drill. Ike and I made a driver change, Don Fritz and big Bob Pero refueled the car, but changing tires was not with NASCAR precision. We had one quick impact gun and a socket and ratchet. Must have been a five-minute stop.

We kept going like this for 500 miles, finished third and won $1,300. WOW! It was exciting.

CHAPTER 24

Turning Professional IMSA/FIA

I called Lee Gaug, the man in charge of sports car racing at Goodyear Tire after our great finish at Brainerd, Minnesota in the UnCola 500 and asked if he would support us also with free tires in the professional series known as IMSA. He replied most certainly.

Two weeks later we went back to Brainerd, Minnesota also known as Donnybrook and ran the IMSA race. Ike put us on the pole. Donnybrook was a fast track. The first two turns were wide open! Holy Toledo, hang on baby! While leading the race, the $200 Chevy big block said adios.

In professional sports car racing, the fastest series was the Can Am for unlimited engines and innovation. The leader was McLaren; they built their own engines, and they were not for sale. The engine supplier for the Lola cars was George Foltz. It just so happened that he and my mechanic, Todd, had gone to high school together. I did not have six grand, so I learned something from Orv Heil when I worked at Toledo Sign. On Fridays if Orv could not make payroll after grousing about people not paying on time, he would walk down to First National Bank and float a 30-day signature loan.

I walked into my bank, the Lucas County State Bank in the Colony, and asked my banker, Tom Taylor, for a 30-day note to buy a racing engine. If you have good credit, no problem. A week later we were installing a Foltz Can Am engine in our Corvette. Putting a Can Am 470 cubic inch finely tuned engine in a Corvette was like putting a jet engine on your bicycle! Next race was the IMSA Mid-Ohio six-hour race. The headline in Competition Press was "Ike and Mike leave the international stars in the dust!" Ike qualified us two full seconds faster than the next fastest car. It was an incredible feat.

Ike Knupp was an engineer at American Motors and drove the factory AMX in B/P when we met him. He was highly skilled. The first time he drove our Corvette he noticed a jacking sensation in the turns. One night he brought two suspension engineers to my shop, and they determined the solution was to change the rear suspension geometry by adding a half-inch aluminum spacer between the gear housing and lower control arms. It made a huge difference in the handling in the turns.

Mid-Ohio was not a high-speed track. You made your time in the turns, but the big engine would put bus lengths on the competition on the long straight away.

"Gopher" Bob Mowery had obtained his SCCA National Competition license and entered our former Shelby GT 350 Mustang. After qualifying he came and told me they had not qualified fast enough. In most races one had to qualify within 110 percent of the fastest car. They had to run a 10-lap race, and the top three cars would transfer to the six-hour race. Would I drive the car for him? I started sixth out of ten cars. I drove the wheels off the car and picked up two seconds over my fastest time ever at Mid-Ohio. Gopher and his co-driver, Dr. Carl Armstrong, were in the race.

The morning of the race, Ike and I rode around the track sitting high in the back seat of a convertible waving to the crowd because we had earned the pole position. We were rock stars! Ike started the race and was leading when the fan belt pulley broke. He pitted, and we did not have a spare. The Holiday Inn Corvette had dropped out and was pitted next to us. They graciously let us have theirs and replaced ours. We lost 16 laps making the repair. Ike went back out, put the pedal to the metal and started the long process of making a next to impossible comeback. It started to rain. Rain and slick racing tires don't work very well. He brought the car in for Goodyear rain tires and fuel, looked at me and said, "Murray it's your turn." Our car had no top, I had experience racing the Mustang in the rain, but that car had a roof. I had to tiptoe on the wet track with the powerful engine. In the rain you accelerate slowly so you won't spin out. I passed many cars and was only passed once and that was by

Jerry Thompson in the Owens Corning Corvette. Jerry would later co-drive with us at the Daytona 24-hour race in 1973.

We finally realized we could not get a good finish and parked the car after completing 165 laps out of 182. It was better to save the car and engine for another day.

After the race Bobby Lumm came up to me and said what a masterful job I had done when it started raining. He watched our car spin off the straightaway at high speed, do a 360, return to the track and keep going. I said it was not me. Ike never told me about that one. When I asked about it later, he just smiled.

CHAPTER 25

I Once Had Nine Lives, Now I Have Eight

The FIA (Federation International Automobile) at Watkins Glen, New York was one of the most prestigious sports car races in the world. The six-hour endurance race was once held on the streets of this small town, but a challenging newer road racing circuit was in its place. The Murray Racing Team had never been there before. I hesitated to send in our entry because I had another kidney stone and the previous one had required surgery. I wanted to wait and see if I could pass it. If I had to have surgery, I would not be able to drive for a while. I passed the stone about two weeks before the race, sent in our entry, but could not find a motel room anywhere close to the racetrack. This was a very prestigious race and attracted spectators from around the world. Sometimes you just must figure things out after you arrive.

Todd Hammitt, our ace mechanic, and Kathy McMurray were married on Friday night. Bob Haube our crew chief, and pilot rented a new (20 hours) Cherokee six-passenger airplane for our 6 a.m. flight Saturday morning to Watkins Glen. Over Cleveland our radios jammed, and the emergency homing beacon went off. With the radio on all we heard was "wo, ah, wo ah." The FAA rules said we should turn around and go back to Toledo Express airport, but we had a race to go to. We had sponsor commitments and had sent the rest of the team on ahead with the car, truck, and trailer. It was cloudy; all we could do was to use the VOR navigation system (flying to and from a high frequency homing beacon) to Watkins Glen airport. We circled down from 5,000 feet (about the length of 15 city blocks) through the clouds (scary) and homed in the VOR beacon. The altimeter said 1,000 feet (about the height of the Empire State Building) and the mountains were 2,500 feet (about half the elevation of Denver, Colorado). We were hopscotching through the valleys looking for a visual of the airport when the engine died. Yes, died, dead, quit!

Haube yelled at Todd to move his feet, so he could play with the fuel tank switches on the floor. We had plenty of gas in both tanks, but the engine was not getting fuel. No one panicked aloud. My stomach was in my mouth, my heart racing. Six, eight, ten seconds later the engine fired. When your radio is not working you circle the airport tower counterclockwise to signal them that you have no radio communication. We landed and left the plane for repair. We were told because the emergency beacon was going off, the civil air patrol was out looking for us.

We were assigned a garage space and parked our tow truck behind it. We did not have a motel room. The team brought sleeping bags and our usual cooler of baloney and peanut butter, baloney and cheese, and ham and cheese sandwiches. Do not laugh. We were racing on a shoestring. Today the big teams bring their own chefs and sit at tables with tablecloths.

Ike qualified us on the pole position in the over 2500cc class by almost two full seconds and 15th overall. Ferrari had three factory cars in the race including America's top driver, Mario Andretti.

The team arrived on Friday, set up our garage and spent the night sleeping in the truck, on top of the truck cap, under the truck and in the garage. Sunday, I remember Carla Marlett slept in her sleeping bag on the hood of the race car. We needed a shower, but there were no facilities at the track. Watkins Glen is in the Finger Lakes region, so we headed out to a nearby lake. I knocked on a cottage door and asked permission for the team to take a bath in the lake in front of their home. I received a strange look, but we really had no other choice.

Permission granted. That water was so fricking cold even though it was mid-July. Here were eight of us taking a bath in bathing suits in knee deep water. Besides freezing our butts off the soap did not want to rinse off.

I was sleeping on a shelf in the back of our pickup truck on Sunday morning race day when I heard chanting and a unison response. It was 6 a.m. when I was awakened by the Ferrari Team coming to work marching in formation coming towards our truck. They were an awesome sight. Four abreast and at least ten rows deep. They were wearing red berets, yellow T-shirts, khaki shorts, work boots and knee socks.

We had a mechanical problem and did not start the race.

The team took the race car home, and I flew with Bob Haube, Todd, and Kathy. The mechanic at the Watkins Glen airport checked out the plane and found no problems. We had a beautiful, smooth flight home.

Two weeks later, that plane dropped out of the sky after taking off from Toledo Express Airport at Airport Highway and Albon Road. The pilot and passenger were killed. I said a prayer for them and thanked the dear lord it was not us.

Bob was a witness at the FAA hearing six months later. The new plane had a clogged fuel filter.

CHAPTER 26

First Time Racing at Daytona International Speedway

The last IMSA race in the 1972 season was the Presidential 250 at the mecca of American racetracks, Daytona International Speedway. It was my first time at this magnificent facility. I was in awe at how large it was. I felt like I was walking on hallowed ground.

The main reason the Murray Racing Team came was to prepare for the upcoming FIA 24 hours at Daytona in January. We broke the shifting linkage early in qualifying. Ike had no first or second gears. Todd made the repair. Ike started the race in sixth position, our slowest qualifying position to date. The race was 66 laps. Our fuel calculations told us there would be two pitstops at 25 laps each leaving 12 laps after the last fuel stop.

The race started, and Ike only made four or five laps when the linkage broke again. He knew he had to stay out for 12 laps to stay in a two pitstop sequence. He came in for the repair and topped off the fuel at lap 13. We lost three laps before he made it back out. He was not out five laps when it started to rain. Everyone else came in for rain tires but Ike. He knew he had to stay out for another 20 laps to stay on schedule and had three laps to make up. Using his wits, he ran up next to the wall in the dry and tiptoed through the infield wet portion of the road course on slick (smooth, no tread) racing tires. There was no chicane (a sweeping left, right, left turn) at turn three at the time. The chicane was installed in 1975 to slow the cars down. He drove wide open all the way around the high bank and slowed for turn one to go into the infield portion.

His next pit stop was at lap 38, rain tires and fuel. He was back out quickly. The team was doing great tire changes; we only needed one man doing the refueling. BIG Bob Pero, Sparrow as I called him, was 6 feet 5 inches and weighed better than 300 pounds. He played tackle at Central Catholic High School in Toledo and college. He was strong as an ox. (Sparrow was in seventh heaven whenever we found a buffet restaurant.)

Ike was back in with 12 laps to go. We finished the race in seventh overall and fourth in class, only one lap down from the leader. Ike put on a clinic in how to drive a sports car in both wet and dry by lapping the entire field twice.

When we returned to Toledo, the first thing we did was to take apart the entire car in preparation for the 24-hour race in January. Kate Friess was our team mother (Kate often brought a delicious dessert to the race shop and made our four dozen sandwiches for race weekends); we called her mom.

Kate was cleaning the radiator; she noticed that the bottom 30 percent of the radiator was clogged with bits of rubber. In a long race the radiator could become completely clogged and the engine would overheat. Race tires wear off little balls of tire rubber. Where does it go? All over the track, in radiators and is blown up to the outside of the track. Don Fritz replaced the grill with two varied sizes of screen, a quarter inch, and half inch about an inch apart to deflect the rubber tire balls so they would not get stuck in the radiator.

In 1975, Carl Armstrong, Fred Guy, Rollie Early and I flew down to watch the 24 hours at Daytona. About 10 hours into the race, I was standing in the pits, and I noticed the Al Holbert team was pulling the engine out of their Dekon Monza. I walked down the pit wall and asked one of the crew members what the problem was. He said, "It's overheating." I said check and see if the radiator is clogged. Sure enough.

As an aside ... We flew in Friday night, arrived at our hotel, and checked in to our hotel rooms. Rollie and I were hungry. We were walking from the hotel to the IHOP directly across the street and were intercepted by two hookers who asked if we wanted a date. "No, we're not interested but you might want to ask Carl and Fred, they're in rooms so and so." We walked away and split a gut we were laughing so hard.

CHAPTER 27

Racing at the Daytona 24-hour Race 1973

When you own a sports car, you dream of racing at Daytona, specifically the most important, prestigious endurance race in the USA and only second to the 24 hours at Le Mans, France. This was my dream and was about to become a reality.

Lee Gaug from Goodyear Tire called and offered me $6,000 to use their tires at Daytona and $3,000 for the Sebring 12-hour races to help them develop their new radial racing tires. John Greenwood was racing the BFG radial Trans Am tires and Goodyear was not going to upstaged. They were the largest racing tire manufacturer in the world. Goodyear was putting the Murray Racing Team Corvette, Roger Penske Team Porsche with Mark Donahue and George Follmer, Brumos Porsche Team, with Peter Gregg Hurley Haywood and the Heinz, McClure Team (Confederate flag Corvette) on the newly developed radial racing tires. Jerry Thompson, the former Owens-Corning Corvette driver, called, and he had Marathon Oil money for this race. He would bring the engine if he could co-drive with Ike and me. My head was spinning; we had made the big time!

In 1973, there were only two garages at Daytona, the Champion Spark Plug garage and the Holman and Moody garage. Our mechanic, Todd Hammitt, was working at Champion in the research and development department. Guess who was in the Champion garage? Murray Racing Team of course! Roger Penske's team had the Holman Moody garage.

The rules required each driver to complete 10 laps of day and 10 laps of night practice, and all drivers had to qualify within 110 percent of the fastest car. I had not driven here before, so I picked Ike's brains on the braking and shifting points. Of interest was the back straightaway and driving the high banked oval turns through three and four. (There was no chicane (a sweeping left, right, left turn to slow the cars down) aka the Bus Stop on the back straightaway until 1975.) He said, "Don't lift your foot off the gas all the way from turns 2, 3 and 4 until turn 1 and hang on for the wildest ride of your life. You will go into turn 3 about 190 mph. Stay low when you hit the tunnel bump in turn 4. Grit your teeth, it will move you up a car width and scare the daylights out of you!" If Ike can do it, I can do it! Holy Toledo, what have I gotten myself into?

Jerry Thompson had the fastest qualifying time for our team. We were second in class and seventh overall on the starting grid out of 55 cars entered. The Tony Delorenzo Corvette won the pole for our class and started just ahead of us. We were the fastest of the Goodyear-sponsored teams and out-qualified the Penske Team factory Porsche by two full seconds. The fastest BFG Greenwood Corvette started seventh in class and 18th overall. Goodyear was pleased.

The race started with Ike behind the wheel. Green flag was in turn 2; Ike was up to fifth overall before he got to turn 3. Fifty laps into the race, the engine dropped a valve. We were done for the day. Huge disappointment to say the least.

We packed up and went to the hotel had a good meal and slept soundly.

Sunday morning, we went back out to the track with four hours left in the race and watched cars drop out after running 20, 22 and 23 hours and determined that if you are going to break, break early. I cannot fathom the pain of staying up all night in the cold, pit stop after pit stop. Driver change after driver change and dropping out close to the end of the race.

I learned an important lesson in life when I was a senior in high school. I did not have a healthy year. I had my tonsils out, appendix out, mono and an auto accident. My Aunt Katie Gray took me home with her to help me get healthy again. Her only daughter was married so it was just Aunt Katie, Uncle Bill, and me. She fed me vanilla milkshakes made with cream and eggs, steak, and Fanny Farmer chocolates. One morning it was raining, and the waves were in high in front of her home on Maumee Bay at Edgewater Drive. I was making my bed when she walked into the room and I made the mistake of saying, "Isn't it a rotten day?" Little five-foot-one Auntie put her finger in my face and said, "Be grateful, count your blessings, you've got two arms, two legs, you can see, hear and talk. I don't ever want to hear you say that again." Yes, ma'am! Trust me I heard the lesson and to this day every day is the greatest day ever. I am grateful.

Sure, we were unhappy that we did not do better. It was a chance to shine. It could have been worse. This lesson has stayed with me all life. As a salesman, I have disappointments all the time, a lost sale or something out of my control derails a sale. You must let it roll off your back, pick up the pieces and move on. There will be better days ahead.

CHAPTER 28

Sebring 12 Hours, 1973

The first time I went to the 12 Hours at Sebring, Florida was in 1967. I saw Mario Andretti win the race in the yellow Ford GT40 MKIV. I never dreamed I would be racing there six years later. The 12 hours at Sebring, Florida was the second most important sports car endurance race in the USA. We pulled Jerry Thompson's Daytona 24-hour engine out and put back our George Foltz 470cid racing engine.

Ike was good friends with Bob Tullius of Group 44 racing fame. Great guy, awesome driver, he agreed to co-drive with Ike and me. This was the first time Ike had ever seen the Sebring racetrack. With little practice he qualified us third on the grid. There were no prototype cars in the field, just pony cars over 2,500 liters and under 2,500 liters. Ike started and was leading the race at the two-hour mark, right after a driver change to Bob Tullius, when he lost oil pressure in a sweeping turn and blew the engine. I saw our car coming down pit road with oil dripping beneath the engine.

I stopped in Columbus, Ohio, after being up all-night driving back from Florida and took the Ohio Real Estate examination. I had not opened the book to study for two weeks. I was tired and was not expecting to pass. I received a passing grade of 70 ... whew by the skin of my teeth!

CHAPTER 29

IMSA Six Hours at Mid-Ohio

W e had no more big block Chevrolet engines, and I could not afford to buy a new one. Sitting in the corner of our shop was the small block B/ Production engine that John Greenwood had built for us when I bought the car in 1971, two years earlier. The engine had six races on it. The B/P 350cid engine was somewhat restricted for the class it ran in SCCA. Hydraulic lifters, cast iron intake manifold and a Rochester carburetor. Maybe 300 horsepower.

Todd put the engine in, it fired right up, and off to the six hours at Mid-Ohio we went. I felt just two drivers were needed so I asked Alan Barker, five-time SCCA National Champion in B/P, to co-drive with Ike. I had a good time teasing Alan throughout our years on the SCCA national point circuit. He had a Kentucky accent and I said he talked like a hillbilly. LOL, he was a software engineer at IBM.

Sunday race day, the team was up and opened the Holiday Inn restaurant at 6 a.m., in Mansfield, the closet hotel to the track. The team strived to always be the first up to eat, first car out to practice and the first car on the starting grid. Alan sat next to me and ordered breakfast: two eggs over easy, sausage links, hash brown potatoes and wheat toast with two extra eggs on the side and a cup of raw onions (true story). The chef made a mistake and sent out two complete breakfasts. Alan said no problem and scooped all the food on one plate. He had six sausage links, four eggs and a double order of hash brown potatoes with four slices of toast on a side plate. He poured the cup of raw onions on top and proceeded to cut everything up with a knife and fork to mix it all together. He then peppered it black. He cleaned his plate and even ate the four slices of toast with jelly. I was in awe! I had never seen anyone eat this much for breakfast not even "Sparrow" Bob Pero. Alan was a normal size six-foot man, too.

Ike had another amazing qualifying session. With that little engine we started third on the grid. We did have a small advantage over all the big block Corvettes in the race. The engine was lighter and achieved better gas mileage. We made two fewer pit stops and that saved a lot of time. After six hours we finished in second place, our best finish on the IMSA profession circuit. Time for a celebration!

As an aside ... whenever we raced at Mid-Ohio, Bob Haube would fly his little Cherokee 4 passenger plane to the racetrack. We would watch for him to make a low circle around the track and throw out a roll of toilet paper, so we would know he arrived and go pick him up at the airport.

CHAPTER 30

IMSA 5OOK at Watkins Glen 1973

It was an eight-hour drive to Watkins Glen, a small town nestled on the beautiful Finger Lakes Region in eastern New York State. This was our second time racing at this legendary road racing course. We were still using our 350cid small block engine that had six SCCA races and the six hours at Mid-Ohio on it. It was still purring along.

We were due for a win after finishing second at the Mid-Ohio six hour in June. Ike had another of his great qualifying runs and put the Murray Racing Team/Greenwood Corvette third in our under-powered car on the starting grid. We had a good start and about lap 50 Ike was going through a blind turn and came upon a slower Porsche and rear-ended it. The front end was heavily damaged as you can see in the photo. He brought it back to the pits and the crew assessed the damage and went to work cutting off the severely damaged front fenders, spoiler and grill. We used bailing wire and duct tape and only lost three laps. Ike wanted to stay in the car. He was really upset and poured the coals to it. With about 100 laps to go he had unlapped himself three times and put the damaged MRT black Corvette into the lead.

John Bishop, the owner of IMSA, came down to our pit and informed me the Peter Gregg (factory Porsche) filed a protest because we did not have complete body work. John was not going to stand for it. He asked me to make a blanket of duct tape and put it over the front fenders on our next pit stop, then he could argue that we made a second attempt to repair the car and would deny Gregg's protest. We did as we were instructed.

With 12 laps to go we were still in lead and were ready for our last pit stop when our car failed to come around the track. It ran out of gas on the pit in lap.

Except there will come the day when the car doesn't arrive . . . and in an instant, the monumental pressure of an entire weekend is gone . . . as is victory

Watkins Glen Program

"Except that there will come a day when the car does not arrive and in an instant that monumental pressure of an entire weekend is gone as is victory."

The picture and words above tell the story. Jim Flickinger (L) Michael Murray(R) We were devastated when the car did not come in for the pit stop.

CHAPTER 31

Gopher Mowery

I found this photo of my Greenwood Corvette from 1972. Our first pro race, the UnCola 500, 1972 at Donnybrook Raceway in Brainard, Minnesota.

Pictured is "Gopher" Mowery. (Go for this, go for that) Bob Mowery, aka "Gopher", showed up at our race shop at 2216 Tedrow in Toledo, Ohio, one day. He was 17, a high school senior, drove a red Mustang fast back and wanted to be a part of a racing team. He had no skills. We took a liking to him. He had no father and no siblings. We took him in and taught him about life and mechanics. We taught him personal hygiene, proper dress and how to polish his shoes. You know, the kinds of things big brothers do. We also found him his first date.

I found him a job sweeping floors at Lakeport VW. When he was 19, I told the General Manager, Bob had the personality to be a salesman. Bob got a promotion and in 6 months was top salesman.

Bob married, moved to California, and died in a tragic motorcycle accident in the desert at age 30. Everyone loved our gopher. I miss that kid and think of him often.

CHAPTER 32

The End of My Racing Career

My dear friend Verne Armstrong once told me, "It is better to have dreams go unfulfilled than to have no dreams at all." My dream was to be able to make a living driving and owning a sports car racing team. I also had a great group of team members who shared that dream with me. The countless hours, blood, sweat and tears we all put in ... we gave it our best and left our mark.

We had a great deal of success in our two years on the IMSA and FIA professional circuits in 1972 and '73. A rag tag team from Toledo, Ohio, who slept eight in a motel room, ate peanut butter and baloney sandwiches left their mark on Corvette Racing history. No one knew we were racing on a shoestring. We competed with the best and often beat them. We always wore uniforms and looked the part of a successful racing team. Why, we were even trendsetters! Gopher Mowery talked me into bell bottom white Levi's one year.

In the nine professional races we entered, we either qualified first, second or third or finished first, second or third, eight out of nine times. To the best of my knowledge, we were the first Toledo team to compete in the big three American sports car endurance races: Daytona 24-hour, Sebring 12-hour and the Watkins Glen 6-hour races. No other team that I am aware of from Toledo has accomplished this to date.

I want to thank my teammates for their loyal dedication and incredible memories: Todd Hammitt, Donald Fritz, Ed Boblitt, Rich Speith, Carol Kolbeck, David Friess and younger brother Bill Murray. I will never forget the commitments of those that have died. RIP Bob Pero, Jim Flickinger, "Gopher" Bob Mowery, Bob Haube, Kate and Sandy Friess. My heart still aches at their loss. I loved them all.

Several years ago, an old friend I worked with at American Custom Shop showed up at a car show I regularly attended with a Corvette Racing History hardcover book. There was our photo and a brief description of the Murray Racing Team. I felt fulfilled. He asked me to autograph his book.

The racing world took a big hit in 1973 when the OPEC oil producing countries quadrupled the price of oil. This produced a gasoline shortage and sometimes long lines at the gas pumps throughout the world. The media did not think it was fair for racing teams to waste gasoline for sport. The handwriting was on the wall. It was time to move on to a new career. I had stopped in Columbus, Ohio, on my way home from Sebring in 1973 and took and passed the real estate license exam.

CHAPTER 33

My New Career

I sold my bus bench business in 1972. I took the Ohio real estate examination on the way home from the Sebring 12-hour race in March of 1972 In the summer of 1972, I began my real estate career as a rookie agent at Melle Real Estate on Byrne Road in Toledo, near Glanzman Road across from the former Frisch's Big Boy. My daily driver was a green Volkswagen bug. I sold a home to out-of-town customers my first month and never looked back. Stu and Mary Hodge were my first sale in the Crossgates subdivision near my office. We looked for two days. In and out, in and of the bug. They never complained.

My sales manager was a trip. Ron Steiben was his name. He used to say to me, "Murray, what did you sell today? We need the money." I was the legs for two older agents who did not like to show homes. I was hungry. They would set the appointments and I would show the homes and write the contracts. One woman was an incredible "matchmaker." Delores Perlman knew our inventory of homes down to a tee. A buyer would call, tell her what they were looking for, and Delores would match them to the perfect home. She would tell them to bring a check and a fine young agent would meet them to show the house. I did not have to do any selling other than ask them, "Is this the home that is talking to you?" It worked like a charm. We would split the commissions. I sold a million dollars' worth of real estate my first year when the average sale price was $28,000 a home.

I worked with Gary Sloan at Melle; he was a top salesman. Gary was a year older than me. He listed four new homes on Ramm Road in Whitehouse, Ohio and was having a difficult time selling them. Finally, he sold one and took a house in on trade. 1503 Holloway Road in Holland, Ohio, was about to be my first home. The attraction ... a three and half car garage. I needed a place to store my race car and equipment, so I could close the MRT shop. I was married in 1970 to Martha, we had two children Amy and Todd. I also wanted to get out of my apartment since I had two small children. I did not have much money. Gary said that since I was an employee and buying a home to live in, I would not have to pay the" house share" of the commission and he would give me his commission also. He was hot to sell the trade-in. I went to the commercial loan department at the Lucas County State Bank and borrowed $7,000 on a 90-day note for the down payment, then I went to the mortgage loan department for a $21,000 mortgage loan. After closing costs, I walked away from the closing with about $1,200. I went in the office the next day. Gary came to my desk with an envelope that had $1,000 cash inside. I said, "What's this for?" He had put an extra $1,000 in his asking price in case he had to carry the house for three months. Since I bought the house right away, he did not have this cost and wanted me to have it. Wow! What a kind gesture.

Gary was a mentor while I was a young salesman at Melle. About eight years ago, I ran into Gary walking out of a restaurant, and he stopped to say hello. I took this opportunity to thank him again for helping me get started in the real estate business and for his gift of a $1,000. He was taken aback and smiled. Whenever I run into someone who helped me climb the ladder, I go out of my way to say thanks. Gary died from cancer a year later.

After I got my feet wet as an agent, I realized that the top company in the Toledo area was The Danberry Company, but they would not hire rookies. My next goal was to become a Danberry agent. I did not have to wait long, Tom Salsberry, the VP, left Melle Realty to open a Westgate office for Danberry in 1974. He asked me to join him. The average Danberry office at that time had 12 agents. I felt honored to be asked. Danberry was a cut above. Coat and tie whenever in the office, button down collars and your shoes had better have a spit shine. All men were expected to dress like the owner, Richard C. Glowacki a Yale MBA. He was a class act and drove a Mercedes-Benz or a Jaguar. I hit the road selling and made the Million Dollar Club two more years in a row and became a lifetime member of the Million Dollar Club. When he found out my racing background, he would not go to a race when invited unless I went with him, so I could tell him the inside scoop about what was going on. He and I became good friends. I loved Dick, he was great to work for, I felt bad when he retired and sold the company.

CHAPTER 34

Characters I Worked With

I worked with two characters in the Westgate office. Jim Breneman, aka "Spinner." In the early 70s, the State of Ohio passed a law that made it illegal to roll back automobile speedometers. Dealers were the worst offenders. "Spinner" had a steady account of Cadillacs coming to the office a couple times a week after the law was passed. You could always tell a Cadillac salesman when they would come in the front door and asked for Jim. Frumpily dressed, overweight with ill-fitting suits and their ties were not straight. "Spinner" would take them out the side door, go to his car and take out a small toolbox, get in the Cadillac and disappear behind the Sheraton Hotel directly behind our office. Half hour later Jim would be back and come in the door with a smile on his face. He was a good guy and a great salesman.

I cannot mention the other agent's name. Let us call him Joe Smith. In a real estate office, agents take floor time: 9 a.m.–Noon, Noon until 3 p.m., 3 p.m. to 6 p.m. and 6 p.m. to 9 p.m. That agent would get all the leads that came in during their floor time. Joe loved 6 to 9 p.m. and would often trade for your 6 to 9 p.m. He liked to go drinking after he got off floor time. I asked him one time if his wife minded him coming late at night. He said she was sound asleep and did not know how late it was when he got home. "You had to know just how to sneak in without waking her up." "How's that I asked?" Quietly come in the house, get undressed before you go upstairs, shoes in one hand and your clothes draped over the other arm. Slowly walk up the outside out the stairs one at a time. If you walk in the center, the stairs will creak. Once upstairs quietly set your clothes down inside the bedroom, slide one foot under the covers slowly, then slide all the way in. Worked like a charm. A week later I went in the office and there was Joe with a big knot on his forehead. "Jesus Jenny, what happened to you?" I asked. "She was waiting for me in the dark as I rounded the corner in the bedroom last night and hit me with a frying pan." LMAO! True story.

One time I heard Joe taking a phone call from a bill collector. "Listen here, I get 12 bills a month, I put the names in a hat and pull out six, do you want to make the hat?"

CHAPTER 35

The Dream House

I sold my first home on Holloway Road after I sold my racing equipment and redecorated it. Martha and I had an amical divorce. I made a nice profit and bought a beautiful English style three family at 1317 Laclede in West Toledo behind the library on Sylvania Avenue in 1975. I lived in the upstairs unit. One year later I bought another three-family next door at 1321 Laclede.

In 1977, I bought my dream house at 2210 Robinwood Avenue in the Historic Old West End. I first spotted this home when I was a little boy visiting my grandma Murray, who lived a block away on Virginia Street. This stately eclectic style brick and limestone English Tudor home was at the corner of Robinwood Avenue West

Bancroft Street in the Historic Old West near downtown Toledo. It once was the home of John North Willy, the owner of the Overland Car Company. Today we know it as Jeep. Every time I drove by, I said to myself ... someday I will own it.

My opportunity came in the summer of 1977. I was taking an appraisal class at the University of Toledo and my instructor, Dick Hunt, asked to speak to me after class. He wanted to tell me that he referred me to the Oblate Fathers of Mary Immaculate, who just happened to own my dream house. The Oblates had lived there since 1937. He had just appraised it for them, and they planned to sell it. This order of Oblates were chaplains at hospitals and taught at high schools in the Toledo area; their numbers had dwindled and the few that were left were moving back to Boston.

I did not wait for a phone call. I went there the next day, rang the doorbell, and introduced myself to Father Donavon. After walking through it, I had second thoughts. It needed a total redecorating. The woodwork throughout the home was natural, but the kitchen's four rooms were painted white. The main kitchen had no base cabinets, just white metal set in cabinets and a porcelain cast iron sink.

The interior was painted early Catholic, salmon, grey and light green just like their schools.

The hot water heat boiler was oil heated and there were no storm windows or insulation. It took a nudge from my wife second wife Ellen. We bought it. I went from an 1,100 square foot apartment to an 8,700 square feet (about twice the area of a basketball court) home on three floors plus and an attic and a basement. Two bedrooms to nine bedrooms with 7 1/2 bathrooms and four gas fireplaces. It had character and charm. Stained glass, leaded glass, quarter sawn golden oak, mahogany, cherry, and chestnut woods throughout. The former ballroom had been converted to a chapel with four altars, six pews and hand-painted liturgical symbols on the beamed ceiling. It took a good 10 years of sweat labor and many dollars to renovate it.

The first thing I did was to convert the oil heat to gas heat. My January gas bill was $1,100. February, the same. Yikes! When spring came, we insulated the attic (14 inches) and added 144 storm windows. The neighbors went together and made a bulk buy of two energy saving devices for boilers. I was first in line.

I hired a friend, Karl Armstrong, to play Santa the first Christmas. He had one condition, beer and cookies, no milk. LOL! The beautiful 10-foot Christmas tree was in the foyer. We put the children to bed, ages seven, five and four. I snuck Karl up the back stairs to change into Santa on the third floor. He had bells on his feet. He walked down the back stairs to the second floor and peaked in each child's bedroom. They were pretending to be asleep. After he was downstairs putting their presents under the tree, we let the children get up and watch him through the spindles of the railing on the second-floor landing. Not a peep was heard and eyes this big.

The next day on the way to Grandma's, the littlest one said, "Hey, that Santa was black!"

CHAPTER 36

Living in the Old West End

I became an active member of the Old West End Association, then president in 1979. The OWE is a real neighborhood made up of black and white, rich, and poor, gay and straight people. Everyone is treated like neighbors and friends. It was a wonderful experience meeting and friending people from all walks of life. Artists, musicians, professional and blue collar. The common goal was to save these historic homes. The extra plus was enjoying a high quality of life through friendship and comradery.

We did have a crime problem just like all areas of Toledo; however, we did not just sit around complaining. For two years we lobbied Toledo City Council to increase our police protection and hire more police officers to no avail. We would call the police for various problems and sometimes they were short of units to assist us. We finally took matters into our own hands and formed a non-profit named Old West End Security (OWES). Our group was Judy Stone, John Czarnecki, Greg Knott, Murray Whiteman, Vicki Koelsch, Eileen Goeke and Tom Quinn. We had our first organizing meeting in my dining room January 21, 1981.

The plan was to organize 12 blocks with a block watch program augmented with a private security patrol to be the eyes and ears for Toledo Police Department. A block meeting was held in each block. Each block captain's job was to explain the program, sign up neighbors and collect the money. Neighbors were taught how to secure their homes and watch out for their neighbors. Just the presence of a patrol car driving up and down the streets was a crime deterrent. We started by asking each home and business to contribute $15 a month for a 90-day trial. Each homeowner that joined was given a special sign for their front window. Over 300 homes signed up. We interviewed several security companies and chose Minuteman Patrols.

Judy Stone was the volunteer resident manager and coordinated between the residents, the patrol, and the Toledo Police Department. April 1, we rolled it out. The news spread like wildfire with the local media. Radio, TV, and newspaper wanted to know what we were doing. We cut our crime drastically.

If someone was caught committing a crime in the "'hood" we sprang into action and lobbied the prosecutor., adult probation or anyone that would listen. We gave support to victims when needed in court. We provided input before sentencing and sometimes met with the judge. The best part was the day of sentencing. I asked a defense attorney one time what he would advise his client when he found out that I and a bunch of OWE neighbors were going to be in court for his day of reckoning. He would tell his client to bend over and kiss his ass goodbye!

One of our worst criminals was Kevin Carte; he lived in the 2700 block of Glenwood Avenue. He stole a neighbor's car and was caught. Kevin was no stranger to the court-house. He had a lengthy record, so we knew with some OWE pressure on the system Kevin would spend a few years playing rock hockey in the state prison. We packed the courtroom. Judge Christenson asked Kevin if he got a fair trial. Kevin said no, his public defender did not call all his witnesses. Kevin was caught red handed in the car he stole. Got it!

The judge sent for his public defender to explain. While waiting, the judge had Kevin read his arrest and conviction record into the court transcript. "Tell me about the bike you stole … Tell me about break in …" This went on and on for about 20 minutes. I thought we were going to be there all day. When the judge asked about the package of baloney he stole from the Kroger store, I could not contain myself any longer. I burst out laughing. My wife pinched my thigh and gave me the "look."

Finally, the judge had heard enough. His attorney told the judge that Kevin had given him no names to call. Judge Christenson sentenced Kevin to two to five in the penitentiary.

This was a victory for the neighborhood.

Three or four years later, my young son Todd and I were taking a walk on Robinwood Street and stopped at the crosswalk at Delaware Street when I heard someone behind me calling my name. "Hey, Murray," I turned and saw Kevin Carter about 20 yards behind me. Oh my! Fortunately, we were taking the Minuteman Patrol's security dog, Luke, for a walk. Luke was the biggest, baddest, blackest German Shepard you have ever seen. Luke only knew his commands in German, but I felt if Kevin got hostile, Luke would take his head off. I was wrong.

Kevin had his hand out to shake mine. He wanted to thank me getting him to straighten up his life. He had been paroled and was serving an apprenticeship at Sun Oil in Oregon, Ohio. He was very gracious. One year later he referred his mother to me to sell her home on Glenwood Avenue.

In the two years that I served as president, our batting average was five arrested, five convicted, five went to jail. Once the perp was in jail, the block captains organized a chain letter for all the people on their block to send. It read, "Crime don't pay in the Old West End, pass it on!" I would follow up with a custom-made T-shirt as a gift from the OWES officers that said. "Crime don't pay in the OWE M___ F_____, pass it on!"

We cleaned up our neighborhood. Old West End Security is still operating 41 years later.

CHAPTER 37

"Life in the Hood"

S ometimes bad guys live in the neighborhood and sometimes they are just passing through. I lived at the corner of Robinwood and West Bancroft, I also owned all the way to the corner of Scottwood. Kitty corner from my driveway was a 12-unit apartment building. There was a basement apartment with the door facing Bancroft. A woman was living there. I noticed one day a lot of people going in and out, cars stopping, beeping their horn and she would run out and make a quick exchange. I realized that she was selling drugs. That did not sit well with me, so I called the police, the mayor, the DEA, and the landlord to no avail. This went on for several weeks. One time I saw her leave her apartment and go for a walk. It was dark. After she rounded the corner, I snuck across the street and emptied a tube of super glue in her door lock.

Next time, I glued not only her lock but the hinges as well. She did not get the message. I finally resorted to taking photographs of the cars that stopped license plates.

One Sunday morning I was washing my motorcycles in the driveway and saw her come out of her front door and walk towards me. Hmm, what is this all about? She walked up to me and got in my face and asked why was I harassing her? I told her that this was a family neighborhood, and I did not want any drug dealing going on by my home or anywhere else in the neighborhood.

It continued. One evening I saw a drug sale going on right out in the street in broad daylight. The buyer was driving a late model Chevy. I wanted a good close photo of his license plate, so I walked closer on the sidewalk. He turned his head towards me and looked out his window. He did not look happy. I walked back towards my house. I had my photo when he started backing up towards my driveway. There was a large bush between me, his car, and the gate to the backyard. Sitting at the gate was our 140-pound Rottweiler, Pasha! Pasha was a bad ass, mean, junkyard dog. I used to walk him down to Rally's hamburger at Monroe and Bancroft on his birthday and buy him a triple. He ate it in one swoop. The dude could not see me behind the bushes walk over, open the gate, and walk Pasha back over the sidewalk. By this time, his car was backed into my driveway, and he was getting out. Then he saw my big dog and me. He just stood there half in and out of his car.

"What's your problem man, why are you taking my picture?" I walked closer and had my hand on Pasha's collar. I was not worried about this druggie attacking me as long I as had Pasha by my side. I told him I was taking pictures for the police department of the drug buyers across from my house and it was in his best interest not to come over here to buy his drugs anymore. He left in a hurry.

I put more pressure on the landlord by calling her repeatedly. The tenant finally moved out.

CHAPTER 38

The Historic Old West End

Toledo's Historic Old West End is the largest concentration of Victorian and Edwardian homes ever put on the National Registry lock, stock, and barrel at one time. There are over a thousand homes in this district. Included is Toledo's world class art museum and magnificent churches along Monroe Street and Collingwood Boulevard.

In the early 50s when the interstate highway was carved out through Toledo, it took out the southwest corner of the neighborhood. The state bought homes for demolition to clear a path for the highway.

This started the decline, but it was not until the early 70s that urban home dwellers returned. The city zoning allowed the large mansions to be turned into apartments.

When I bought my home in 1977, I thought I was buying a home to raise my family in. Little did I realize my family would soon become many neighbors. The first winter was the blizzard of 1978. We were stranded for a week. Neighbors got on the phone and organized a "picnic" at my house. People loaded their children on sleds, cleaned out the refrigerator and we had a wonderful time.

The OWE Festival is the highlight of the year. A two-day event that starts with the Scott High School marching band leading the parade. A half a dozen neighbors work all year long preparing homes that will be featured on the home tours. There is delicious festival food, an art show and yard sales in every block. Many neighbors have annual parties throughout the weekend to entertain family and friends from outside the neighborhood.

I believe in 1995, I was asked to bring my Harley-Davidson Motorcycle Chapter to ride our bikes in the parade. We had about 30 bikes parading along with the floats and marching band. After the parade all the bikes parked in my driveway along Bancroft Street, so the neighbors could stop by and admire these gleaming chrome machines.

That afternoon, a newspaper reporter approached me from the Toledo *Blade*. She informed me that she heard there was grumbling among members of the gay community about the Harleys in the parade. We were stereotyped as being the dredges of society once again. I explained that we were the doctors, lawyers, and Indian chiefs and sponsored by Harley-Davidson. I could not believe of all people; some gays would discriminate against us. I was quoted in the next day's edition in the Toledo *Blade* Newspaper as saying, **"We are doctors, lawyers and Indian chiefs ... and we don't eat our young."**

Every Christmas the women of the OWE organize Tours de Noel, a Sunday afternoon event with beautifully decorated homes open to the public and caroling in the OWE Commons Park.

This is a special neighborhood where neighbors are a real family. One time a family fell on hard times financially. A group of neighbors put together an auction. They cleaned out the basement, bringing a treasure to the Murray house on a Sunday evening. My broker at the time, Tom Salsberry, was the auctioneer. We raised $5,000 to lend a helping hand.

We had another neighbor whose husband had MS and could no longer climb stairs. Their extended family built them a new ranch home on the family farm. They needed to sell their existing home, but the Victorian home's outside needed a fresh coat of paint. No problem. Twenty-five neighbors showed up and spent two weekends washing, scraping, and painting their home. It was like worker bees building a hive. A two and half story Victorian home is not the same as an average home in a suburban neighborhood. We had a festive party. Many brought ladders and paint brushes. Other neighbors brought food and drink. It was incredible, just like an old-fashioned Amish barn-raising 75 years ago out in the country with many people helping.

I will cherish forever my 21 years living in the OWE.

CHAPTER 39

Taking on the Toledo *Blade*

BLADE PHOTO

Through my interactions as an advocate for the Old West End, I became acquainted with the mayor, city manager and city council members. In the mid-80s, the mayor called and asked me to represent neighborhoods in the cities three-quarter-percent income tax renewal campaign. I gave a speech in support of the renewal at the kick-off in Promenade Park along with John Anderson of the Andersons in Maumee who represented business support; the unions and seniors were also represented.

We all worked diligently in our areas of expertise to gather support. The three-quarter-percent tax represented about 25 percent of the city's total income. If the levy did not pass massive layoffs would occur.

On the Thursday before the election, the Toledo *Blade* newspaper came out against the renewal. They supported five other tax levies but not the cities. Unbelievable how reckless the *Blade* was in their lack of support. Naturally, everyone at city hall was upset. I received a call from the mayor's office informing me that a mass protest was being organized by the city employees especially the unions at noon in front of the Toledo *Blade* building on Monday at noon. Being the rebel that I am, I made a picket sign over the weekend and was looking forward to Monday's demonstration.

I usually started my Mondays at the Lucas County Auditor's office doing real estate research. On Monday, at 11 a.m., I went up to the mayor's office to check in. Mayor Owens explained that they had been looking for me to tell me they had cold feet and called off the protest in front of the *Blade* for fear of the *Blade's* retribution. Hey, I made a cool picket sign and felt strongly that the newspaper was wrong and wanted to have my voice heard.

I was the lone picket walking in the front of the *Blade* building on a very cold and windy Monday. People driving by blew their horns in support. Others gave me the thumbs up. I felt like a rock star. Suddenly a *Blade* reporter, Eric Bates, who was also my neighbor on Robinwood Avenue, confronted me. With his notepad in his hand, he said the bosses upstairs wanted to know what I was picketing for. I said, "Read my sign, Eric," and then proceeded to explain my position. When the interview was over, he asked if he could bring me a hot cup of coffee. I said, "Sure, blond and sweet." He said, "I will bring it from Portside after lunch." "What, I was hoping that you were going back inside, fix me a coffee right now. It's cold out here." He said, "Do you want me to get fired for giving you a cup of the Blade's coffee?"

Sue Duckworth (assistant city manager Mike Duckworth's wife) was driving by, stopped, and asked if I was hungry. She brought me a White Tower double butter burger 😊.

As I walked by the corner of the building, I noticed a photographer in a *Blade* blue jacket sneaking up on me trying to catch me in an awkward poise. "Hey, you don't have to sneak upon me for a photo. Take your best shot. Is my tie straight?"

My friend, Kathy Brandman, who was the receptionist at the front desk, told me later that someone remarked about the protester out front. Kathy came to my defense and said, "At least he's a classy picketer, wearing a suit, tie and wearing wing tipped shoes."

I was about to call it a day when a *Blade* employee approached me. He told me the employees in the print shop took a straw poll and the levy would pass.

Tuesday, on election evening, I celebrated with many others at the city's election party. We the people won. The levy passed.

CHAPTER 40

Strong Mayor vs. Council/Manager Government

I n the mid-80s, the city lost $19 million that was invested in a Florida fund named ESM. A few heads rolled because the loss represented 25 percent of the city's investment fund. The Toledo *Blade* newspaper saw this as an opportunity for a power grab and advocated for a return to the strong mayor form of government. Toledo did away with a strong mayor more than 50 years earlier. In a city with only one newspaper, the publisher would control who and who was not elected. If you chose to run for elected office, you had to kiss the ring of the publisher. A non-elected person would be in control of the local government.

With a council manager form, professional managers with degrees in Public Administration would manage the city. A city's primary duty is to provide safety (Police and Fire), refuse collection, safe water, and sewers for sanitation. In a strong mayor form, most administration jobs are used as political spoils for party hacks who worked on the campaign of the strong mayor. They were not the least bit qualified to be department heads.

The city manager arranged a lunch with his assistant managers and me. The *Blade* was bound and determined to put the form of government change on the ballot. The city manager felt that it would be self-serving for him to try and defend the form of government that he represented. He asked me if I would form a committee to oppose the *Blade*. I did not have to think twice about my decision. I believed that Toledo was better served with professional management. I was honored that he asked me.

I asked my friends Susan Hauenstein (president of the Woman's League of Voters) and Jim Godbey, attorney, and political strategist, to assist me. We formed Concerned Citizens for Toledo. While we were organizing, city council was considering putting the change on the upcoming ballot when wiser heads prevailed and convinced the council to form a Citizen's Charter Review Committee to study the issue and bring back a recommendation to the mayor and council. The esteemed John Stoefler, the dean at the University of Toledo law college was appointed chairman.

Six months later, the committee recommended no change. The Democratic-controlled council came up with the excuse, "Let the people decide." I am sure there was pressure from the *Blade*. The battle lines were drawn. The *Blade* formed a group of movers and shakers to push for strong mayor led by George Haige, president of Toledo Trust Bank, Toledo's largest and oldest. We were not intimidated!

The *Blade* started writing stories daily advocating for the change. When we were interviewed, they distorted our position or buried it in the back pages. I finally resorted to excluding them from our press conferences. I was holding a press conference in my dining room one morning when the non-invited *Blade* reporter just walked in the front door. He did not even have to courtesy to ring the bell. I got up from the table and showed him the door. LOL. All three TV stations were there and recorded me throwing him out. I made it very clear that if you do not report fairly, you will get no cooperation from me. The reporter made a big mistake because the news of his forced exit went wall to wall on radio and TV, 12 noon, 6 p.m., 11 p.m. and 6 a.m. the next day. It was the lead story; we had the issue and the people on our side. It was David vs. Goliath.

We raised a great deal of money anonymously from citizens who were afraid of the *Blade*. If you run afoul of the Big Bad Newspaper, they would eviscerate you on the front page. They could not do anything to me other bad mouth me and I did not care. I was fighting for a just cause.

Jim Godbey was a brilliant strategist. He designed a full-page newspaper ad that had a large picture of a chair in the center. The headline was, "AUCTION We the People vs the Toledo Blade Newspaper and Toledo Trust Bank." I wanted the ad to run on the Thursday before the election. I knew the *Blade* would not run the ad, so we set them up. I had many copies of the ad produced and planned with six weekly papers to pick it up with a check (all political ads are paid up front) at 5 p.m. on the Wednesday. At 1 p.m. I walked into the *Blade* with the ad and a check. John Murphy, the classified ad manager, came downstairs after the bosses looked it over for 45 minutes. John said, "Michael, we can't run this ad, you cannot say 'We the People.'" "Why not? I looked up the word in the dictionary and it means more than one." I gave him my bottom line: He had until 4 p.m. to change his mind or I was going to run the ad in all the weekly papers and have a press conference in front of the *Blade* at 9 a.m. the next morning and it would be the lead story and go wall to wall on radio and TV..

Four o'clock came and went so I followed through and called a press conference for 9 a.m. The weekly papers picked up the ad and their checks. About 7 p.m. John Murphy called and said, "Michael, I've known you a long time, let's meet for breakfast tomorrow and talk about it." "Sorry, John, you missed the 4 p.m. deadline." I had no time to waste. The election was next Tuesday, He just wanted to stall me.

Thursday morning 9 a.m. the press conference was held right outside the *Blade's* front door. I had the ad blown up and mounted on a large piece of cardboard sitting on an easel. Not only did the ad run in the weekly papers, but we also got free TV and radio coverage. The TV cameraman focused right on the ad for all to see. Again, we had wall-to-wall coverage at noon, 6 p.m., 11 p.m. and 6 a.m. the next day, five days before the election. The International City Managers association brought in six city managers including Cincinnati, Phoenix, and Dallas, etc., for a press conference the day before the election.

"We the people" won on Tuesday. The *Blade* pressured city council to put it back on the ballot two years later and we won again. They put it on the ballot a third time and "We the people" lost. It is my opinion that the city of Toledo has never recovered.

CHAPTER 41

Name the New Newspaper Contest

I n the mid-80s, in the aftermath of one of the council manager victories over the *Blade's* push for strong mayor government. Mayor Donna Owens and City Manager Phil Hawkey were being interviewed. A TV reporter stuck a microphone in my face and asked my thoughts. I blurted out, "Toledo needs another newspaper." The next day my phone lit up with strong financial support and many people agreeing with my words. Concerned Citizens for Toledo regrouped and laid plans to bring another newspaper to Toledo.

The brilliant political strategist Jim Godbey suggested that all we needed was a Toledo supplement to another large city paper, local news and sports, obituaries and classified ads as a pullout section.

Newspapers such as the *Detroit News, Cleveland Plain Dealer, Columbus Dispatch,* or the *Cincinnati Enquirer* would be good candidates. But first we should commit to a four-week public awareness campaign followed by a short survey by a reputable polling firm. This survey would provide a base for our sales presentation.

We embarked on the four-week "Name the New Newspaper Contest" aimed at school-aged children with a grand prize of a pizza party for the school of the winning student. It was a sure way to involve their parents and raise awareness. We ran coupon-style ads in all weekly papers and kicked it off with a press conference. We received wall-to-wall media coverage; even the *Blade* showed up and ran a story.

The coupon had space for three suggested names and was to be mailed to a post office box. We received over 10,000 entries. The most popular was the *Frog Town News.* At the end of the campaign, we held another press conference in my dining room and spread the entries out on my 10-foot table. It was impressive. The *Blade* sent a photographer who tried to get closeups of some of the names on the entries. I moved him back away. I did not care if he took a distant shot, but no closeups where they could read the names.

A prominent citizen paid the $7,000 cost of the survey. It was a simple four-question survey. The two most important questions were, "If a new daily newspaper came to

Toledo would you subscribe?" and "If you bought a subscription to the new newspaper, would you cancel your *Blade* subscription?"

You know the answer; it was overwhelmingly in favor of support for the new newspaper and a certain cancellation of the *Blade*. Godbey wrote a letter, included the survey, and sent to the papers we had identified. He then followed up with a phone call and found the *Detroit News/Free Press* were salivating at the thought of a hundred thousand new customers and wanted a meeting as soon as possible.

The date and time were set only to have a cancellation at the last minute. We were taken aback. Later we were told by an anonymous source that the *Blade* found out about our meeting and threatened the *Detroit News* that they would start another newspaper in their backyard.

We were not successful but surely enjoyed poking the bully in the eye.

CHAPTER 42

Career Opportunity

In 1979, I was ready for a sales manager's job. I did not see any upcoming opportunities at the Danberry Company. There were two real estate companies that were looking for sales managers.

Cavalear's Perrysburg office was new and first class. They had a good staff and were selling about a million dollars' worth of homes a month, which was the norm in those days for a top-notch office.

Neal Realty, on Monroe Street, also had an opportunity. This office only had $166,000 in sales the previous month. The staff were not well trained, and the previous manager was not successful. Most agents were relatively new. My apprehension came from the owner's reputation. He would build the sales staff up and then they would leave. I interviewed him six times. I liked the challenge of training a group of eager salespeople. I took the job at Neal with one caveat. The owner had to agree to hire an Industrial Psychologist to figure out why agents left.

The psychologist was hired and after a week of interviewing the administrative and sales staff he returned his $5,000, one-sentence report: "Owner picks pepper out of fly shit."

I went to my first management meeting and was called aside by the manager of the south office. He said he had an agent that wanted to transfer to my office because it was closer for her. He had no objection if I wanted her. He went on to say that she was new and had been there for six months and had not listed or sold a house. She also had to take the real estate exam four times before she passed, and he did not think she could make it in real estate. Bingo! She took the test four times and never gave up. This woman had a rare quality. I told him to send her over.

There are three kinds of people in this world: those that make things happen, those that watch things happen and those that wonder what happened! Marita Deitering made things happen.

The next day she came in for an interview. She is a German immigrant, married with three children under age 10 and was working as a nurse but really wanted more flexible hours and a better income.

No wonder she had difficulty passing the test. Try taking the real estate exam in a second language. She was determined to succeed, and she did. I told her I would make a commitment to teach her the real estate business if she would make a full-time commitment and leave her other job. She agreed and would give her two-week notice.

I told her that she could start in two weeks. She started crying. "What's wrong?" I asked. "I was let go from the south office this morning." *Mmm* "Where's your briefcase?" "It's in the car." "Go get it and you may take the desk over there." Several weeks later Marita was taking floor time and excitedly she came back to my office. "Michael, a man walked into the office and wants me to list his house. What should I do?" "Ask him if we can come over at 4 p.m. today or would six be better." I helped her do the research on the home and get prepared for her listing appointment. Marita listed the house. It sold quickly, and she sold the gentleman another home. She was off and running and never looked back. She quickly became a top agent, made the million-dollar-club, and went on to become one of our best agents. Besides being truly knowledgeable, she possessed excellent communication skills and most importantly her clients knew that she cared about them.

Our office was humming, and we had our first million-dollar month in sales within the year.

My little sister Mary wanted to become a nurse. Mary went to McCauley High School and a nun told her that she would have to pass chemistry to become a nurse. Then she proceeded to tell Mary that she was not smart enough to pass the course. I cannot believe someone would squash another person's dream like that. Mary did not listen. She was determined to succeed and make her dream come true. She passed chemistry and went on to a lifelong career in nursing. Sadly, she died a year ago.

"If you can dream it, you can do it." I have lived my whole life making my dreams come true. If someone tells you that you cannot do something, do not listen. Just do it!

CHAPTER 43

The Art of Baking

In the spring and summer of 1991, I went through a life crisis. Ellen and I divorced after twelve years of marriage. My life has had difficulties just like everyone else's, and I struggled to go to work every day. I did not eat well and lost 27 pounds. Getting through each day sometimes took all the strength I had. On top of that I fell and broke my left wrist.

My daughter Amy was going back to college in August so before we left for Central College in Iowa, I asked her to teach me how to make cupcakes since I had a sweet tooth. We went to the Kroger store and bought a cake mix, cupcake rounds and a can of frosting. I could not believe how easy it was.

A client bragged about her mother's cherry cobbler and never fail crust. One day she taught me how to make it. Another friend had a Bailey's Irish Cream cheesecake recipe, so we made it.

When you are in a life crisis you can choose a constructive passage or a distractive passage. I choose a constructive passage. I started baking. It was the best therapy. As an artist I was a natural. I had an idea for a Christmas dessert party. Since my ex-wife Ellen took all the Christmas tree ornaments, I decided to have an ornament party to fill my bare 10-foot tree.

I bought a heavy-duty mixer, baking pans and several dessert cookbooks and started baking and freezing.

Close to Christmas I designed a simple invitation that read, "Brand new bachelor has a berry bare tree. Bring me an ornament for my tree and I'll feed you a dessert from around the world." I sent over a hundred invitations to my Christmas open house.

My children, Amy and Todd, and a few friends helped me assemble it the day before and the day of the party. Every dessert was made from scratch, including frostings, cookies, pies, cakes (six), candies and cheesecakes (nine). I also made calligraphy name cards for each desert. Twenty-five different desserts were awaiting my guests.

We put up the tree several weeks before and strung over 2,000 lights.

The evening of the party, I barely left the living room. My guests were a steady stream of family and friends. I unwrapped each ornament and placed them on the tree. The party was a grand slam home run.

I had so much fun, and it was so therapeutic for my soul that I held the party the next Christmas also. The second year I made 35 deserts from scratch.

When you are down, you need to pick yourself back up.

My mother and grandmother were great bakers and taught my sisters the art; they were even better than Mom. Several years ago, my little brother Dave had a family baking contest. It was a big event. He even brought in expert judges. You guessed it … Michael won the grand prize. ☺

CHAPTER 44

Toledo Chapter
Harley Owners Group First
Charity Motorcycle Show

I n the fall of 1993, we asked our members of the Toledo Chapter Harley Owners Group to nominate their favorite charity to be the recipient of the proceeds from our first MC show. Six groups made a presentation. My good friend Ron McCance brought a 22-year-old named James Wilhelm, a resident at the Cherry Street Mission. Jim was a recovering alcoholic and drug addict. He was picking himself up by attending Owens Community College and obtaining a degree in Culinary Arts.

James made his presentation, he was shy, he shook with nervousness, and we could barely hear him speak. He asked for $800 to pay his next semester's tuition. He had completed one term and had three more semesters to graduate. We liked the fact that he was picking himself up; he was determined to succeed, and he was chosen.

We thought the Franklin Park Mall would welcome our show, but we were wrong. Just because we rode motorcycles, we were the dredges of society in their eyes. No problem. Southwyck Mall in South Toledo rolled out the red carpet. The three-day show was held on the first weekend in February 1994. Our members brought over a hundred gleaming Harleys to the show. That was a challenge because the weather was bad. Members with trailers assisted others without. It was truly heartwarming to see the effort everyone put in to make our first show a success. Sylvania Harley-Davidson donated a $500 leather jacket for our raffle prize. We put on a good ad campaign and the mall was packed.

We had planned to sell tickets throughout the weekend but sold out on Friday night. We put a large fishbowl on the ticket table and asked for donations. Our goal was to raise $800. We were pleasantly surprised at the end of Sunday to have over $4,000 in our fund for James Wilhelm.

Our agreement was to donate one semester of tuition worth $800. Instead, we could pay the last three terms of his schooling and as a bonus, we would buy his books. All he had to do was pass each term and stay clean.

The day of James's graduation, many of us were in the bleachers with pride in our hearts. We took a chance on a young man, and he came through for himself, family, and friends. I will never forget this day.

After the ceremony, the Toledo Chapter Harley Owners Group gave James a check for $1,100, which we had left over in his fund to help him get started and leave the mission he had called home.

But wait there is "more to the story."

Several years later Ron McCance and I were in Sturgis, South Dakota, when Ron received a call from Jim. He was getting married and asked Ron, the minister, to perform the ceremony. I went with Ron to the wedding that was held outside at Secor Park on Central Avenue, west of Sylvania, Ohio. We rode our Harleys and wore our finest leathers.

After the wedding Jim insisted, we come to the reception at the VFW Hall in Delta, Ohio. We had planned on going riding after the wedding, but Jim twisted our arms.

We were in for a surprise. We were shunned by most of his guests. We felt uncomfortable and decided to eat and leave quietly. Jim noticed that were exiting and stopped us and stopped the band and took the microphone and then proceeded to shame the wedding guests for the rude treatment of his friends just because we were bikers. He went on to tell them that he was a broken man once upon a time. Ron, Michael, and the Toledo HOG Chapter lent him a helping hand. He would not be there today if it were not for these two men and their kind generosity. There was dead silence. He told them how we paid for his education and gave him a large monetary gift at his graduation. He then asked them to honor his special friends. They gave us a standing ovation. We stayed and were treated royally.

Jim went to work for Mancy's Steak House as a cook in the kitchen.

"Never judge a person by what they wear, you never know what's in their hearts". Michael Murray

CHAPTER 45

My Dream Job

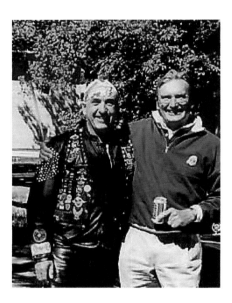

I left the Danberry Company and took a sales manager position and as a vice president at Neal Realty in 1979. We had the office humming along and were setting records every month when the bottom fell out of the real estate business in the recession of 1980–82. Interest rates soared to 17 percent. I hung on for a year then had to make a change. I saw no relief in sight. I had a wife and three children to feed and educate.

I had an offer to go to work for a real estate and securities broker. I would still be able to sell homes in the Old West End while obtaining my Registered Reps and Securities Brokers licenses for limited partnerships. During the first year I had both, then found out the owner was dishonest with our largest client. I did not want to be associated with a dishonest employer. The timing was right for Tom Salsberry, my former broker at the Danberry Company, to entice me to return. I went home to Danberry a smarter wiser agent.

My ex used to say I could sell the panties off a nun! I love sales and love bringing new people to the Old West End. From 1984 through 1991, I was in the top three in sales and listings year after year at the Danberry Company. I do not think I ever missed being in the top 10 overall at year's end.

In 1991, Mr. Glowacki called and asked me to become a vice president and take over managing the Danberry Oregon office. My dream had come true. That office showed a steady decline in sales for the previous five years when the market was particularly good. I was ready for another challenge.

I met individually with each agent to get to know all about them and what their sales needs were. I heard loud and clear that they wanted training and a manager to be there for them. I had a great staff and just needed to inspire and train them. I was a full-time manager and gave up selling. I loved these agents and gave them my best. They treated me like a king. I instituted a weekly training program and they started producing results. We even had a 4-million-dollar sales month.

At the same time, I was getting into riding my Harley. When you ride a Harley, you need to have the Harley persona. One day after our managers meeting, Mr. Glowacki called me aside and said that the senior managers were going to mentor the junior managers. I had only been a VP for two or three years. I went to a private mentoring session a week later. Big Fella, aka RCG (Richard C. Glowacki), started telling me about a Russian war general who was going into battle and instead of confronting the enemy head on, he went around them and avoided the conflict. I was saying to myself, where is he going with this? Then he comes out with it ... a total blindside. Do you remember when I told you in an earlier chapter that RCG expected his agents and managers to look and dress a certain way? Proper dress was suit, button down shirt collar and tie, wing tip shoes, very straitlaced, after all he had an MBA from Yale. My earring was bothering him. "It was totally inappropriate for a Danberry VP to wear an earring," he said. I was dumbfounded. I said, "Dick, you knew when you hired me that I dance to the beat of a different drum." I was in a position of strength because my office was one of top producing offices month in and month out. I politely told him I was not removing my earring. End of story.

Whenever Dick invited me for a round of golf at the Inverness Club a high brow country club, I always made sure my golf shirt sleeves covered my tattoos (wink, wink).

One summer I rode my Harley to our annual management retreat at his summer home in Walloon Lake, Charlevoix, Michigan. He asked to have his picture taken with me. Yes, I was wearing an earring.

Dick was great man to work for and with. He was brilliant and built one of the most successful real estate companies in the Toledo area. He was a man of integrity and left his company in the hands of two men just like him, Lynn Fruth, and Dick Baker. I still miss him and think of him often. He retired in Florida and recently passed away. I loved that man.

CHAPTER 46

Halloween at the Opera

I dated the *Blade's* music critic, Willa Conrad in the mid-90s. Willa had a master's degree from Peabody as a music critic. She was beautiful and smart. I went with her to classical music venues in Toledo, Cleveland, Ann Arbor and Detroit. She wrote her reviews in the car on her laptop on the way back to Toledo.

I always wanted to go to one of these highbrow events in my finest Harley black leathers. The opportunity came to attend opening night of the opera season at the Fisher Theatre in Detroit. This was a fundraiser and black-tie affair. Tickets were $500 to see the Barber of Seville, my first opera. We did not have to pay, and she did not mind what I wore.

She wore a long black gown under her mink coat. I was leather from head to toe. A red native American long bandana cut off gloves and sunglasses. We had to pick up our tickets at the will call window. She stood in line facing the window; I stood next to her facing the crowd as if I were her bodyguard. LOL.

We had sixth row seats. She sat in the end seat, so she could hear better. The elderly woman sitting next to me told me about their experience watching the parade of Harleys going to the Harley-Davidson 90th anniversary ride a few years earlier. I did not even frighten her as I have done when in the presence of others.

During the intermission, we were enjoying a refreshment when a little boy about 10 years old and his sister came up to me, tapped me on the arm and held out their hands. They each gave me a piece of candy and said, "Nice costume, mister."

It was Halloween.

CHAPTER 47

Niki Vasco's Make-a-Wish Ride

In 1995, I received a call from Rebel who rode with a Christian Riders group. Rebel had served 10 years on an Alabama chain gang. He found religion while in prison and learned the leather craft. His shop was on STR 2 just outside of Archbold, Ohio.

He was organizing a Make-a-Wish Ride for Niki Vasco, a 10-year-old boy from Montpelier, Ohio, with inoperable brain cancer. Little Niki's wish was a Harley ride to the Dairy Queen in Bryan, Ohio. He asked me to bring the Toledo HOG Chapter on the ride and some ride pins or HOG patches for Niki's leather vest (colors) he made for him.

Over a hundred Harleys showed up and met in the Montpelier High School parking lot. Niki's mother had him sitting on the tailgate of a pickup truck. There was a long single file line of bikers presenting Niki with pins and patches for his colors. The leather vest that Rebel made brought tears to your eyes. It read, "Child of God" on the top rocker and "Prince of Peace" on the lower rocker.

I presented to him on behalf of the Toledo HOG Chapter an "Honorary Road Captain" patch we had made up just for him.

The ride left Montpelier; Niki's mom was on the back of big Harley dresser with Niki in a side car following a sheriff's cruiser with lights on leading the way. This little guy was all smiles. In true biker fashion, the road captains rode ahead and blocked side traffic, so our parade was able stay together.

We arrived in Bryan, Ohio. The Harleys filled the Dairy Queen, McDonalds, and Wendy's parking lots. It was a site to behold. We made an unforgettable memory for this little boy. He thanked everyone while eating his ice cream. Wow! What a day!

A month later Rebel called to tell me little Niki died, and his mother asked if the bikers would come to the funeral and provide a Harley escort from the funeral service to the cemetery. The service was held in the Montpelier high school gymnasium because of the large, expected crowd.

Niki had four brothers and sisters and their entire classes wanted to attend the service. Niki's mother played the piano as each class sang a child's song for Niki.

I had gotten up and went to the restroom and when I returned to the gym, I saw a hundred plus big bad ass bikers dressed in black, with long hair, beards and tattoos bawling their eyes out singing "Puff the Magic Dragon."

It was a somber parade of Harleys to the cemetery. One could not help but feel the pain of this family's loss and ours too. Niki was one of us.

After the service while still in the cemetery, Niki's mother surrounded by Harleys brought out a boom box and a large handful of Orange and Black Harley balloons. She gave each of her children several helium balloons that they released in the air to the tune of "Get Your Motor Running."

It was very emotional for me to tell this story. I barely knew him, but he is in my heart and all the others that rode that day.

CHAPTER 48

Tit for Tat

I walked in the Danberry Westgate office one day while I was still working as a salesman and found an envelope in my mailbox from Toledo Hospital. I thought that was strange. I had not been sick or been there in while. I opened it while sitting at my desk in the bullpen. In large bold, red letters was stamped "OVERDUE." I read the small print and it was an overdue bill for a liposuction of the chin and stomach. It looked official. Behind me I heard Paul Moburg spitting a gut and laughing his butt off. He had a friend that worked there send it to me. Ha, ha!

A couple of days later I just happened to be at the Franklin Park Mall, so I stopped into Spencer Gifts. I had been trying to come up with a payback for Paul. I spotted a rack of envelopes with just the return name on them. Perfect! I bought them, went back to the office, and started typing.

The first letter to Paul was from the Dingle Berry Shampoo Company. I designed a coupon for 25 percent off a bottle of Fire Hot Shampoo for Flaming Assholes! I sent it to him, and he roared.

A couple of days later I composed a letter from the Small Condom Company that went something like this.

Dear Mr. Moburg,

Thank you for your inquiry and measurements of your rather small penis. I regret to inform you that our smallest condom will not provide ample protection for your little member. Therefore, I am referring you to the Teeny Wienie Condom Company for little dicks.

Warm regards,

Mr. Gotcha Last

I like to tell a good story and hear a good story. I asked Paul one day, "What is the craziest thing you've ever done?" One night Paul went drinking at the Recovery Room, a neighborhood bar on South Detroit Avenue in South Toledo. He had too much to drink so two friends took him home about a mile away. One drove him the other drove his car and parked it in his driveway. He walked around to the back of the house and waited for them to leave. After they left, he came back around and got in his car to go back to the bar. He was not finished drinking yet. He drove no more than three blocks and hit a half dozen cars parked along the street. His car was wrecked so bad he could not drive it. No problem. He walked back home and got his wife's car out of the garage and was on his way back to the bar when he started banging into cars again. This time he walked home and stayed there. Half hour later the police showed up and arrested him for leaving the scene of an accident. He said, "That was nothing compared to what his wife did to him."

Paul was a fun guy to work with. He died about ten years ago.

CHAPTER 49

MDA

O ur first motorcycle show at the Southwick Mall with Muscular Dystrophy Association was an immense success. After we paid for the bike, we gave MDA a check for $9,157.

MDA was our annual charity for 17 years. The Toledo HOG chapter raised over $500,000 during those years for Jerry's Kids. We also gave Harley rides to the MDA kids at camp, which was another home run.

The kids absolutely loved it. I was told that their Harley ride was more fun than Christmas. This small gesture warmed our hearts. Sometimes it took three or four strong men to lift a child out of their wheelchair and put them in the sidecars.

Listening to these special kids say, "Wheee" and seeing those big smiles made it all worthwhile.

There was also a downside. After doing this for several years, we knew who would not be back next year. I attended too many funerals.

At Christmas time we also went to their Christmas party and brought a present for each child.

When Brian Hessel, the MDA goodwill ambassador, age 17, was a senior at Whitmer High. He was confined to a wheelchair; the Toledo Harley Chapter provided an escort for Brian's parents to take Brian and his date to the senior prom in his special van. Six bikes in front of the van and 10 bikes behind. When we arrived at the school, we parked our bikes right in front of the school and escorted Brian and his date into the auditorium. You should have seen the look on the faces of the principal and the students. Brian was an important VIP. We loved Brian.

Brian died March 12, 2012.

CHAPTER 50

My Funeral

October 2, 1994, on my 50th birthday, a dear friend picked me up at the Danberry Oregon office for my birthday lunch. When we returned, I noticed the company sign had been changed to read, "Danberry Funeral Home."

Mmm. As I was escorted into the office, the lights were low, and I could hear funeral parlor music. Mary Ann Coleman, my secretary, placed a sign around my neck that read, "Don't talk to me I'm dead." I then noticed the sign over the conference room had been replaced with my name. As I entered the room, my staff had converted the conference room into a funeral parlor. The conference table was moved to the front of the room and had a wooden coffin laying on top with a skeleton inside. All the chairs were now facing the front of the room just like a funeral parlor. Off to the side was a podium. I tried talking to someone and was totally ignored. I forgot I was dead! All my agents walked in solemnly, heads down, tissues in hand. Bringing up the rear was my blond bomber girlfriend, Kathy Boyer, in a slinky black dress walking arm in arm with my young handsome salesman, Danny Knopp. She was smiling and had plane tickets to Acapulco in her hand.

Randy Brown, the minister in rose-colored glasses, approached the podium and gave his eulogy. The roasting had begun. Several agents took turns poking fun at me. June Aiello, in her finest choir robes, called God and asked if I would be allowed into heaven even though I was wearing an earring.

Permission denied. I was doomed to hell!

While all this was going on, several agents were out in the side yard setting up the cemetery. Tombstones, grass mats, chairs, and old Bill White was dressed as a Harley grave digger.

I had a blast. When my funeral was over, we a had great laugh. I was impressed with their ingenuity and attention to detail. Cake and ice cream were served. I worked with a great bunch people in the Oregon office and will never forget the hard work and fun times we had. I love them all.

My birthday, I mean funeral, is one of my fondest memories forever.

CHAPTER 51

The Enema Nurse

I had duodenal ulcer disease when I was 19 years old. To diagnose my stomachache, it required drinking barium, then the X-rays, then the clean out. While waiting for this procedure in my hospital gown in the waiting area, I saw this beautiful redheaded nurse—tall, thin, great figure—walking towards me. *Mmm*, my lucky day! I smiled, she smiled and walked right past me. In comes this short, obese, dumpy looking nurse in a threadbare uniform, formerly white stockings rolled down to just below her knees, a big pimple on her nose with hair growing out of it and calls out Murray. I said to her, "Oh, you must be the enema nurse?" Then I realized I should not have said that. She replied, "No, we take turns." It was not a pleasant experience especially after I opened my big mouth.

Years later while at Danberry's Oregon office, I was on a Harley trip and found out one of my agents, Randy Brown, was in St. Vincent's hospital for a heart catheter. When I returned, I went up to see him. He was doing okay, and I remembered I owed him one. He was the minister in rose-colored glasses that roasted me at my birthday funeral. The lightbulb went off. I remembered an ad in the Toledo Blade for a plump stripper named Caroline. I called her. For $50, she would pay Randy a visit in the hospital. I asked her to dress like an enema nurse. "No, problem," she said.

She wanted to know if she could do a striptease for him. No, no, this is a Catholic hospital and I just wanted her to give him a hard time. "Can I just bend over and show him my big butt?" "As long as you don't pull your pants down," I said. I told her he was the only one in the room.

I met her at the hospital. She dressed the part, green scrubs and a hot water bottle connected to a four-foot garden hose and nozzle around her neck. She brought a small boombox for a little background stripper music and had composed a poem about enemas.

I stayed behind her and peeked around the corner as she entered Randy's room. Oh my, there was another man in the bed next to Randy. She was quick on her feet and called out. "Which one's Brown?" Randy raised his hand; his bed was next to the window. Caroline in her squeaky voice says, "Roll over, drop them and pucker up, the enema nurse is here!" She pulled the privacy curtain closed, turned on her stripper music, gave Randy some cute one-liners, then read him her poem. A crowd had gathered outside Randy's room, and we were splitting a gut. She was hilarious! She finished and gave Randy a get-well card, then opened the curtain. The elderly Catholic priest in the next bed, sat up and said, "What's going here?" True story, I could not make this up. Caroline takes the hose and nozzle and runs it under her arm pit and tells the priest to "shut up or you're next!"

Wait, wait … there's more … I let a week go by, then had my attorney friend, James Godbey, who had a deep voice, leave a voicemail message for my staff and agents: "Please attend Tuesday's sales meeting. I will read Mr. Murray's last will and testament and bequeath his many assets." I hired Caroline the obese stripper aka the enema nurse to come an hour early. I hid her in the furnace room next to our basement meeting room.

Mr. Godbey welcomed everyone and started the meeting. I walked downstairs wearing a devil's outfit: red Pants, red Harley tank top, horns and a spear wearing my "Don't talk to me, I'm dead sign." It was only appropriate since I had been condemned to hell for wearing an earring. Jim introduced and willed Caroline aka the enema nurse to Danny Knopp, the handsome young salesman who took off with my blond bomber girlfriend to Acapulco. Caroline turned on her boombox to play stripper music, came out and shook her big butt for Danny and sat on his lap.

Randy Brown received the hot water rubber bladder with hose attached compliments of the enema nurse.

June Aiello, who condemned me to hell, received a bottle of red-hot anal shampoo for flaming assholes.

Bill White, the Harley grave digger, received a package of generic condoms for cheap fuckers.

Finally, Mary Ann Coleman, my closing secretary who organized my funeral, a bouquet of flowers.

Everyone had a good laugh.

CHAPTER 52

California or Bust,
On the road again

I drove my Austin-Healey to California in 1965. 1n 1995 I rode my '93 Harley-Davidson Dyna Wide Glide motorcycle to California. My riding friend, Ron McCance, and I set out for the Pine Ridge Indian Reservation and a side trip to Sturgis. Then he was heading home, and I was riding on to California and back solo.

We made a fuel stop in Chicago. It was raining, and we saw two riders from Boston going to Sturgis. They were not dressed as bikers and were not wearing riding gear. They rode a Harley Sportster, which is a small bike. The dude wearing a piece of clear plastic for a raincoat asked Ron how far it was to Sturgis? Ron said, "You guys have about another 1,200 miles." We laughed our butts off at these two yoyos; they were riding to Sturgis in jeans, tennis shoes and T-shirts.

We spent our first night in Albert Lea, Minnesota at a Holiday Inn. There was a softball tournament going on that weekend. We were down at the pool, soaking in the hot tub after a long day's ride and met some of the players. There were coolers of beer everywhere. I met a guy named Joe, the oldest of 10 who farmed 2,000 acres with his family. He was about 28 and was the leader of this team of mostly younger guys. His chest was still healing from recent burns. I asked him what happened? He said someone dared him to slide face first through bonfire coals. OMG! I said Joe, "What's the craziest thing you've ever done besides sliding through a bonfire?" He was out with some young guys one night and they were knocking down mailboxes with a baseball bat. One of the younger guys dared him to stick his arm out the window and take out a mailbox. The driver sped the car up to 50 miles an hour, Joe's arm was sticking out the window, and his arm hit the mailbox and nearly pulled his arm out of his shoulder socket. He toughed it out because he did not want the younger guys to see him in pain. "I've never winced in front of them," he said. "It would hurt my reputation as the toughest SOB around."

The kids took a liking to us and invited us to the tournament party that night. We were celebrities that night because we were bikers, and they wanted their pictures taken with us. Free food and drink.

Ron had met a Sioux Shaman, Everett Poor Thunder, at a Native American Pow Wow at Bluffton College the previous winter. He invited Ron out to be his guest at the most sacred of the Sioux Seven Sacred Ceremonies called the Sun Dance. The Sioux dance from sunup until sundown for four days without food or drink. Ron and I were both interested in Native American spirituality, culture, and art. When I was a little boy, I was always the Indian when playing cowboys and Indians.

We canceled our motel reservation in Rapid City, South Dakota, which we had made a year earlier because we were going to stay at Everett's house in the village of Red Shirt Table, South Dakota, about 50 miles south of Rapid City, South Dakota, on STR 40. We were 180 miles out riding on I-90 when I had a rear tire go flat at about 75 mph. I hung on and brought my bike to a stop. We were 35 miles east of Murdo, South Dakota, home of a well-known auto museum.

We were in a very precarious spot. The east lanes of I-90 were closed for repair and traffic was both east and west on the two-lane portion in the west lane. The road was lined with snow fencing with a pull off area every mile. This area of the great plains is desolate. We had to get off the highway and find a place to take the rear wheel off and replace the inner tube. I was prepared and carried spare front and rear tubes. I had the dealer put new tires on and service my bike before we left Toledo.

Traffic had slowed. We yelled at passing motorcycles asking if they had a tire pump. A Harley brother pulled off and lent us his pump. I sat on my bike, Ron or the other man hand pumped air into the tire. I counted to 60 and fired the engine while they were pumping, then took off and tried to make it one mile to the next pull off area. We repeated this process nine times until the next exit. We were lucky, the first gas station had an old tire and wheel repair shop behind the small restaurant and gas pumps. It had not been used in years, but it had tools and a jack. Ron is an excellent mechanic. It was extremely hot and miserable taking the rear wheel off.

We pulled the inner tube out and found the tube had been pinched when the new tire was installed. It had a one inch slit in it and could not be patched. Ron wrestled the tire and installed the new tube. This took a couple of hours. I went for a test ride and the new tube leaked like a sieve. Ron took it apart again and found five pinholes in the new tube. We patched them and put the wheel back on so I could take another test ride. This time it held air. I had promised Ron a steak dinner in an air-conditioned restaurant for his trouble.

The restaurant where we made the repair was not clean, so we rode about 25 miles to Murdo, South Dakota and found a restaurant with a neon sign that said, "Air Conditioned." We washed up and ate a T-bone steak dinner.

When we came out of the restaurant, the tire was flat. We could not believe it. Ron felt that he needed to ride alone to Everett's home because he knew that his friend would be waiting. He could not call because Everett did not have a phone. The plan was for me to find someone who either had a trailer or a truck, put my bike on and they would take theirs off and drop me off at the Rapid City Harley Davidson dealer for a new tube.

The two small motels were filled, no rooms, but I did find a brother who put my bike in the back of his pickup, and he would ride his bike in the morning. I wheeled my bike across the street to the small gas station and asked permission to park my bike in front of the station and sleep in my bike cover behind the station that night.

I was sitting on a concrete stoop in front of the station in the shade killing time until night fell when a little Yugo pulled for gas. He saw my flat tire. I told him my plans to get my bike and me to Rapid City in the morning. Where are you staying tonight? Next thing I know I am loading my bags in the Yugo.

Whenever I have broken down on the road, it always turned out to a cool experience.

Steve and his girlfriend were house sitting a couple of miles down the road. We pulled in the driveway, and I see a beautiful woman in a string bikini riding a lawn mower. Her name was Star. She had a small star tattooed on her forehead. I took a shower, changed clothes, and sat down to a delicious spaghetti supper. That evening, we sat outside by a bonfire, drinking a glass of wine and smoking a cigar. I slept in an old motorhome on the property. It was much better than sleeping in my bike cover behind the gas station.

The next morning, after a great breakfast, Steve dropped me off at the gas station so I could be on my way. I sent them a thank you gift when I returned home.

CHAPTER 53

The Yuwipi Ceremony

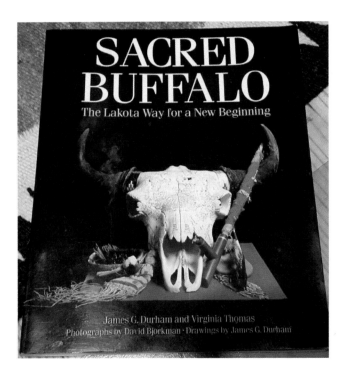

The calling of the spirits is one of Sioux seven sacred ceremonies, at the Pine Ridge Indian Reservation in South Dakota.

On Monday evening during the week of the Sundance, a ceremony was held in Everett's basement. The windows were covered with heavy blankets so that no light could enter. We walked down the steps and standing before us was a young woman holding an abalone shell with burning sage. This was our first time seeing a Lakota ceremony. I brushed the smoke towards me as instructed. The smoke is meant to purify you for the ceremony that was about to take place.

The basement was a clear span with chairs placed in a circle. There had to be 30–40 people seated there. We had noticed during the day many warriors that would dance in the Sundance were making prayer ties. A prayer tie is a piece of colored cloth (black for the grandfather from the west, red for the grandfather from the south, white for the grandfather from the north, yellow for the grandfather from the east, green for mother earth and blue for father sky) that has Native American tobacco wrapped in a circle on the end.

A blanket was in the center of the floor for the traditional healer to sit. Warriors placed their prayer ties, eagle feathers and anything else they wanted blessed on the rug. The Yuwipi ceremony is performed for healing and to find lost items. As an aside, my former wife, Susan, and I were married at the Sundance several years later. Our wedding cake was blessed at a Yuwipi ceremony.

When the medicine man and Shaman are seated on the floor, the lights are turned off and the ceremony begins. It is pitch black; you cannot see a thing. The singing begins, the traditional healer shakes his rattles, and the drum is played. I had a very spiritual feeling; the people are totally into their prayers. Suddenly, I could see a faint white light dancing on the walls. I have no explanation for where it came from. It was not from man. The light signified that the spirit was there.

Everett's mother, Evelyn, is the matriarch of this family. She had the Chanunpa (peace pipe) in her hands. She prayed aloud, then passed the pipe to her left. The next person prayed. The pipe went all the way around the room. People prayed in English and Lakota. They would pray for a job or pray for a sick friend or family member. It was humbling to listen to them. These people were so poor in material things yet so blessed in their spirituality.

The bundle of prayer ties hit me in the chest near the end of the ceremony. When the lights came on, I was told to pick it up, it would bring me spiritual blessings.

Several years later, Ron and I were at the same ceremony. When the lights came on, Everett presented Ron and I with an eagle feather. When I went outside, a young Native American (the grandson of Jay Silver Heals, aka Tonto) came up to me and asked if I realized what a great gift had been bestowed upon us. I told him that I was honored but did not really know the meaning. When you are given the eagle feather, you are given the spirit of a warrior that has passed on. The feather will protect you on your journey in life. I have a story that I will share later.

You will notice the photo of the book Sacred Buffalo. I met the author at Prairie's Edge, a 50,000 square foot trading post in Rapid City, where this magnificent piece of art was on display. James G. Durham had a vision that he would carve in scrimshaw art the bones of a bull buffalo; the skeleton is six feet tall. James and several artists hand carved the Lakota seven sacred ceremonies on the bones. It took seven years. Seven years, that should tell you the enormity of the creative art project.

Scrimshaw art is an art form that is considered by some to be the only art form that originated in America. Sailors working on whaling ships out of New England first practiced scrimshaw art. Designs were carved in ivory and then black ink was rubbed into the design, so you could easily see it.

I am introducing you to this art because we were not allowed to take photos at the Sundance. When I share that story, I will use photos from the book Sacred Buffalo to paint a picture of what we saw.

CHAPTER 54

The Sacred Sundance Tree

On Wednesday evening, final preparations were being made for the most sacred of the Lakota Seven Sacred Ceremonies. Everyone got in their cars and trucks and then rode about a mile to a wooded area. Headlights from the vehicles illuminated the tree. The Shaman selected a tree without stretched limbs to ask the great spirit to have pity on them. A red ribbon was tied around the tree. A young virgin about eight years old wearing a blue dress came forward and made four chops, one on each side of the tree to honor the four grandfathers. The dancers then came forward and took several chops each until the tree fell. It must not hit the ground. The dancers then carried the tree to the Sundance circle. The caravan stopped four times on the return trip to the Sundance site. People got out of their vehicles and bowed to all four corners, honoring the four grandfathers.

When we returned to the Sundance site, the tree was dressed while resting on sawhorses. Large prayer ties were tied throughout the top of the tree and the warriors tied their nylon ropes onto sturdy branches. Once the Sundance started these ropes were connected to the eagle bones on their pierced chests.

A Buffalo had been slaughtered in preparation for the feast on Sunday. Its heart had been removed and placed in the bottom of the hole the tree will rest on. The tree was raised in silent ceremony.

Chokecherry branches were tied horizontally just below the yoke in the tree. Lines in red and blue were painted vertically on the lower part of the tree representing the colors of the Sioux Nation. Warriors then placed small prayer ties around the base of the tree.

The actual picture of the tree was taken on Monday after the sacred ritual on our way out of town.

As an aside, both men and women participated in the Sundance. Women word plain dresses and danced but were not pierced. Men wore loin cloths and were pierced.

In the year before the Sundance, a warrior and the shaman spent a 24-hour fast at Bare Butte Mountain nearby. The warrior drank peyote tea to help him have a vision. The Shaman interpreted the vision and decided how this man would be pierced at the Sundance.

The first warrior I met at the Sundance site was Thurmond Horse. He wore no shirt and had many scars on both sides of his chest above the nipple. He explained that when Native Americans make a vow to the great spirit, they must keep it. His vow was to do the Sundance 10 years in a row if his vow was answered. This was his tenth year.

CHAPTER 55

The Sundance

Four men are pierced to the sacred Sundance tree. When the spiritual man directs them with his eagle-wing fan, they charge the tree four times, breaking free of it on the fourth. Their women, children, and friends support them from the arbor.
Leg: front left (South), middle bone
Page: 140

I was truly honored to be a guest at this most sacred of the Sioux sacred ceremonies in '95, '96 and '97. The Sundance starts each day (Thursday through Sunday) at dawn and ends each evening at dark in a sweat lodge. The dancers dance from sunup to sundown and take a 15-minute break every hour. They also fast for three and a half days, with no food or drink except a little Peyote tea to help with their vision. There is a feast of buffalo meat on Sunday after the ceremony. The Sundance is a tremendous physical and emotional feat of human strength.

This sacred ceremony has been in the Sioux culture for thousands of years. I will let the picture carved on the Sacred Buffalo skeleton tell the story of the rituals during the four days of the Sundance.

I cannot begin to describe the deep feelings of spirituality and being at peace I felt during this time and for days afterward. Even today as I write my memories my spirit within can place me again at the Sundance and among the incredible Sioux.

I continued my motorcycle journey to California. While riding on I- 25 through Colorado, I passed by the Rocky Mountains on my right. I had visions as I passed by each mountain of famous Sioux chiefs Red Cloud, Sitting Bull and Crazy Horse. I will never forget this amazing trip.

My battery died near Steamboat Springs, Colorado. I had ridden in the rain most of the day. If I stopped and turned off the engine the only way, I could restart it was to get a push start down an incline. Once I was rolling, I turned on the engine and popped the clutch with the engine in gear. As I rolled into Steamboat it was dark and pouring down rain. I could not shut the engine off. Motel after motel had no vacancies. I was getting worried that I might have to move on to the next city and I was exhausted. I had one last chance. There was only one motel left at the end of the street. The only room he had was the owner's suite at $250 for the night. That was lot of money in 1995. I was desperate; I talked him down to $150 and breathed a sigh of relief.

I parked on an incline so I could get a rolling downhill start in the morning. It was 85 miles to Grand Junction, Colorado, where the closest HD dealer was located. I prayed the whole way. The dealer took good care of me, and I was back on the road.

Everett Poor Thunder died on January 24, 2014, at the age of 58. His death was a huge loss to family and friends. I will never forget him. Ron asked me to paint a picture of Everett on the fender of his motorcycle as a remembrance of our spiritual friend.

CHAPTER 56

Made It To California

I rolled into Laguna Nigel, California, to visit my godmother, Pat Griffith-Benson. My aunt Pat was the youngest of my mother's four sisters. I always felt Aunt Pat's love. I was a middle child and felt left out when it came to my mother's love. Aunt Pat went out of her way to make me feel loved and special.

She had my favorite lunch waiting for me: mom's potato salad and bread pudding. I spent several days with her and Bob. I then went to San Diego to visit my Aunt Katie and Uncle Dick See. Katie was my mother's oldest sister. She married a navy man and settled in San Diego after World War 2. They also rolled out the red carpet for me.

Her son Steve and I always spent time together whenever I was in California. Steve was about 10 years younger than me and lived in San Luis Obispo, California, about two hours north of LA. One day he took me to the San Diego yacht club to see the America's Cup winning sailboat, the Stars and Stripes. While there we decided to rent a small outboard boat and tour the ships in the harbor. I love warships and planes. We saw battleships and destroyers. It was especially cool to see a ship coming into the harbor with all the personnel in their dress whites lining the perimeter of the ship.

I remembered a time when my daughter Amy was 10. I took her to California to visit my parents (Mom and Dad retired there) and go to Disneyland. We took a whale watching cruise and sailed by the submarine base. I saw several subs from a distance. Here I was 18 years later cruising by the submarine base and thought it would be cool to go in and check them out. There was no sign that said we could not enter. I saw several subs, snapped a few pictures and we went on our way.

We were in the middle of the harbor and were buzzed by a helicopter. It kept going back and forth above us. Steve said, "I think they're following us." We made our way back to the boat rental and I saw the beautiful yachts at their docks. Being a sign painter, I wanted to see the hand painted names on the transoms. We went up one row and down the other taking pictures. As we got closer to the boat rental, I noticed several men laying back in rental boats like ours with their caps pulled over their faces as if they are taking a nap. They were tailing us. We pulled up to the dock and walking towards us were eight navy personnel, two in dress blues and six in fatigues wearing 45s on their belts. I said to Steve, "I think we're in trouble!"

They started giving me a tough time about being in a posted area. I said, "Hey, I'm a sign painter and there was no sign." "If there was a sign, we would not have gone in the sub harbor and besides, I didn't have any photos the Russians didn't already have." They persisted, "We want your film." I argued.

Finally, Steve poked me in the ribs and said, "Give it up or we'll be late for the Padres game." I made a deal; they could have the sub photos, but I wanted the rest of my photos. They agreed.

We made the San Diego newspaper. "Two civilians were caught trespassing in the submarine base" and mentioned our names. Aunt Katie saw the story and told my parents. We got a big laugh out of it.

It took five days on the road to return home. It was a great trip. Several weeks later, I received a letter from the Navy with my film. Of course, the sub photos were blacked out. Steve died on May 24, 2010, at 55 years old. I think of him often, great guy. We had a lot of fun together.

CHAPTER 57

Sly One and the Free bird MC

In 1994, I rode solo to the State Harley Owners Group (HOG) Rally in Marietta, Ohio, which is in southeast Ohio along the border with Kentucky. I was on my way home late Saturday afternoon and had just gotten on the Ohio Turnpike going west when my battery died just before exit 10. Just what I needed; I had an important social engagement early Sunday morning.

Along come four very loud Kawasaki's that flew by me. Next thing I know they turned around and came back. I met Sly One, president of the Free Bird MC (motorcycle club) in Akron, Ohio, his girlfriend, Jade, Bam Bam Free Bird MC and Preacher from the Boogie Down MC out of Detroit. MC means One percenter, could be bad dudes. They offered to help. Sly One said that they had an affiliated clubhouse close to the turnpike exit where they could get a battery charger to recharge my battery. They gave me a hand push. The bike started as I rolled down the ramp to pay my toll. I just got through the tollbooth when the battery died again. Sly One pulled up next to me and told me he was going to give me a straight leg push to the clubhouse.

I had never heard of a straight leg push. He pulled up on my left side, put his leg out straight and hooked his heel to my passenger peg. I put my bike in neutral and away we went.

We were in the ghetto and pulled up in front of the "Zulu" MC. Now I was wondering what I had gotten myself into. I remembered a *National Geographic* documentary I watched about an African tribe of cannibals by the name of Zulus. I had thoughts of my bike getting stolen and the Zulus eating me for dinner. I kept my composure. Sly sent for one of the Zulu members to come and open the clubhouse so they could put a trickle charge in my battery. He ordered Bam Bam to take my battery out from underneath my seat. We had ridden by a Burger King, so I offered to buy burgers and fries for the group. Preacher ran the errand and by the time he returned Bam Bam had the charger hooked up to my dead battery. These guys were great. I was in awe and worried for nothing.

The Zulus had a table and chairs outside between the sidewalk and the curb. We sat, ate and told stories. It was starting to get dark, and I was ready to leave. Bam Bam put my bike back together. I started saying goodbyes and getting addresses, so I could send a gift when I returned home to thank them for their warm hospitality. Sly said, "Oh no, we're going to follow you back to Toledo to make sure you make it home all right." I was dumbfounded. It was a hundred miles to Toledo, and it was 9 p.m. They would not get home until Sunday morning.

It was an incredible gesture of kindness. Sly told me that once we got on the turnpike if my headlight started going dim to pull into the first rest area and they would get a heavy-duty charger from the State Highway Garage and put another charge in the battery. We were on the turnpike, rode past the rest area about five miles when my headlight went dim and the engine died. Sly pulled up next to me and gave me a straight leg push again. He was so close to me that I could feel his mirror rubbing against my left bicep. It was a good 45 miles to the next rest area. He ordered Bam Bam to ride in front and Preacher to ride behind me. We were running 50 miles an hour. I just hung on. This was an amazing physical feat by Sly One.

At the next rest area, they put a heavy-duty charge into my battery, and we were back on the road. It was now near midnight. I was watching the clock because I had to be at my girlfriend's church at 8 a.m. Her father was a minister and was celebrating his 40th anniversary as an ordained minister. The whole family would be there. I had to be there and on time.

We were on I-475 near the Bancroft exit by my Old West End house when Sly One blew a rear tire. Murphy's Law kicked in. It took a while to push his bike to my house.

They took the tire off and left on Bam Bam's bike trying to find a place for a tire repair. I felt this was near impossible. It was 1 a.m. on Sunday morning. I entertained the rest of the group in my kitchen with several flavors of cheesecake I had in the freezer. They returned about an hour and a half later and put the wheel back on Sly's Kawasaki.

I fixed Sly and Bam Bam a piece of cheesecake in the kitchen, so they would not get hungry on the trip back to Akron. It was now 3 a.m. We walked outside to the driveway and another goodbye and Sly's tire is flat! SOB, flatter than a pancake.

We could not believe this day. I had to get to bed, so I produced a plan. Preacher wanted to go to Detroit and Bam Bam had to get Jade back to Akron because she had to work on Sunday. I told Sly I had a guest room with a bath and shower. He could stay the night, there was food in the refrigerator, and I would call my friend George Rogers to come and help him get his bike on the road first thing in the morning. I had to be at the church at 8 a.m.

I was up at 6, called George and he told me he would come at 8 to help Sly One. I woke Sly up and gave him a key to the house. I was home by noon and there was a note from Sly that they had his bike fixed and he was on his way back home. Thank God for good friends.

I invited Sly One and his friends to come to our next HOG chapter meeting. In front of our members, I told them the entire story how these strangers went above and beyond to help a fellow biker. I presented them with HOG patches and made them honorary members of our chapter. I will never forget this story of bikers helping bikers.

CHAPTER 58

The Toe Heads

I rode my Harley to Richmond, Virginia to visit my older brother Jim in the summer of 1994. He was renting a caretaker's house on a 2,000-acre plantation out in the countryside in Goochland County, Virginia. On Friday morning, I rode into downtown Richmond and picked him up at his office building. I was in my finest "scare women and children" Harley outfit, and Jim got on my bike in an equestrian outfit, including the helmet. He is an equestrian. We must have been a sight to see. If there were cell phone cameras in that day, we would have been all over the internet, Snapchat, and Instagram. We were both riding the iron horse.

We rode over to his girlfriend's house, Mary Ellen Bundy. I parked my bike in front of her house. A while later I was looking out the front window and saw four little blond-haired children admiring my bike. I went out the front door to greet them. They saw me and ran away. A brief time later, they were back. This time I caught their attention and they stuck around.

I showed them my Harley and answered there many questions. They were especially interested in the pins on my vest. They noticed my biker's name, "Shoboat." They were well mannered and called me "Mr. Shoboat." I always carried extra MDA ride pins in a pouch behind my seat in the back rest and gave each of them a ride pin. The little boy told me to wait here while he ran home across the street. He was back in a few minutes and gave me his pin to put on my vest. It said, "I'm seven." They were cute kids. They went home and were back in 10 minutes.

"Mr. Shoboat, we're putting on a show in our front yard and we would like you to come and see our performance." *Mmm.* Puts me in an awkward position. What is their mother going to think when this bad ass biker shows up in her front yard with her precious children? They insisted. I walked across the street, introduced myself to mom, and told her I meant no harm, but her children insisted I watch their show. I sat on the ground with the other kids.

The kids had taken a refrigerator box, cut out a large hole and pretended it was a TV. It was sitting in the front yard. They got inside in full costume and put on a play in front of all their neighborhood friends. It reminded me of when I was a kid. We had a picnic table in our backyard and would pretend it was an airplane. My little brother Terry and I took several cardboard boxes and drew circular instruments just like an airplane cockpit and covered the table with a white sheet. We sat on the ground side by side (pilot and copilot) with the instrument panel in front of us. We flew all over the world. Ha, ha!

When their show was over, I asked to take their picture by my bike. When I returned home, I sent a photo to their mom. I wonder what they are doing today.

CHAPTER 59

The Power of the Eagle Feather

I was on my way to Rapid City, South Dakota, solo in the summer of 1996. I spent the night in Sioux Falls, South Dakota. Before I went to bed, I turned on the weather channel. I saw a huge storm was going to pass through overnight. It looked clear after that. I was up early as usual, ate breakfast and noticed it was cloudy and still dark. I thought I should check the weather one more time since I saw no signs that it had rained the night before. Sure enough, the storm had stalled. My choices were to wait it out or ride through it. I am a man and wanted to get there. I had written a letter to Everett that I was coming out for the Sundance again this year the previous January but did not give him an arrival date.

Native Americans live on Indian time; they do not wear watches. Indian time is whenever they get there.

I put on my rain gear, waterproof H-D bibs, coat, gloves, and gators over my riding boots and helmet. I was an experienced rider in the rain. I made my way to the I-90 interstate and headed west. There were five vehicles ahead of me towing Harley's. I referred to them as candy asses. Real men ride! It started to rain. I was in the middle of nowhere; it was the Great Plains. Overpasses were nonexistent and there were very few underpasses. It rained harder. One by one, the vehicles in front of me pulled over to the side of the road until I was all alone. I was afraid to pull over and sit by the side of the road for fear of a car or truck not seeing me and running me over. I turned my emergency blinkers on. Visibility was bad.

I-90 was a four-lane highway. This rain was something I had not been in before. It was a downpour of Biblical proportions. I had slowed to 35 mph from the speed limit of 70 mph and was riding the white line between the two lanes. I learned at motorcycle safety school that your bike goes where your eyes go. I could not take my eyes off the white line. Quite frankly I was in over my head. I kept telling myself to watch the white line and keep moving forward. When the downpour was at its heaviest, a bright light appeared suddenly out of nowhere above and in front of me and lit up the road. It was like one of those helicopter spotlights you see on TV, although there was no helicopter out there.

Those of you that do not know me ... I do not drink or take illegal drugs. My stories are true and not exaggerated. I could not figure out where this light came from. I cannot tell you how long it was on, but it sure lit up the road. I started to look up once, but the helmet was in my way, and I did not want to lose sight of the white line. The storm let up and the light went off.

It was still raining hard. Another downpour happened again, and the light came on a second time. Now I knew I was not hallucinating. I was in awe and kept on riding the white line with the road lit up. When the storm eased up, the light went off and I could see the horizon. Wow! is all I can say. I was impressed by what I had just experienced.

It was another 300 miles to Rapid City; the weather was perfect.

I pulled up in front of the Radisson hotel in Rapid City and sitting on a bench in front was my friend Everett Poor Thunder, the shaman for the Oglala Sioux Tribe. I did not tell him I was staying there or my arrival dates. I made the reservation long after I had written him in January. I said, "How did you know I was going to arrive today and stay here?" All he said was, "I knew you were coming; do you have any of that flavored coffee with you?" I always carry a thermos of Hazelnut cream coffee when I am on the road.

I checked in and Everett followed me up to my room. I poured him a cup of coffee and proceeded to tell him excitedly about the white light and the rainstorm. He listened and did not say a word. When I finished all he said was, "Did you have your Eagle feather with you?" I replied, "Yes, it's in my tour pack." "The feather represents the spirit of an Indian warrior and will protect you on your journey in life." Everett had given me an eagle feather the year before during the Yuwupi ceremony.

CHAPTER 60

Encampment on the Tow Path

O ne of the finest festivals in the Toledo area is the annual Apple Butter Fest in Grand Rapids, Ohio, every October. My good friend Ron McCance set up his teepee along the riverbanks on the tow path along with his brother Dick's and Jerry Eicher's teepees. It was a beautiful fall weekend for primitive camping.

Ron and I rode out Saturday afternoon. I brought my sleeping bag and was looking forward to a fun evening of tasty food, music and sleeping on the banks of the Maumee just like the Native Americans did hundreds of years ago. About 50 yards to the east of us was the military encampment. This was so cool. In between was a camp of settlers including the Galbraith Clan. It was a western movie scene. I remember Jerry Eicher grilling a rabbit on a spit over a small fire in the middle of the three teepees.

As darkness fell, we were sitting in Ron's teepee around a small fire with Ron playing his guitar. We were rudely interrupted by a "rent a cop." He looked like an overweight Charlie Chaplin. He must have been a newbie who had been given a uniform just for the weekend. It was a size too small for him. He had a bad case of "Dunlap's Disease." Oh, you never heard of Dunlap's Disease. You know … his belly Dun lapped over his belt!

In his gruff voice, he says, "Who owns those motorcycles out there?" I said, "Those aren't motorcycles; those are iron horses." "It's illegal to park them on the towpath," said the wannabe officer. "Really," I said. "You'll have to prove to me that an Indian can't tie up his pony next to his teepee." (As an aside, I had painted Native American graphics on both bikes.) He said, "It's right in my law book." "Where is your law book" I said. "In the trunk of my car." "Let us do this, Officer. While you're making your rounds, stop by your car, get your law book and bring it back with you, show me chapter and verse and we can end this discussion."

Did not seen hide or hair of him since our little discussion. (Wink, wink.)

CHAPTER 61

Act of Kindness, Rescuing an Abandoned Dog

everal years ago, we at Pamela Rose Auction Company sold at auction a small strip center on West Bancroft Street in Toledo just East of Upton Avenue. I had an appointment to meet the appraiser there. I pulled into the parking lot and had just gotten out of my car when a Toledo police patrol car pulled in behind me. The strip center was vacant, so I assumed that the officer was just checking me out. I told him that I was the realtor and was meeting an appraiser here. "You're not the reason I'm here," he said. "Do you see that gray blob in the center of the vacant lot next door?" "Yes sir," I said. "That's a stray dog that I came to feed and give water to today." Oh cool. The vacant lot was about the size of an acre of land. He went on to explain that this dog had been abandoned and he had been feeding him daily for about six months. He wanted to catch him and give him a home before winter arrived. The dog has been very elusive and evaded capture repeatedly.

The appraiser showed up, so I left the officer to unlock the doors and turn the lights on. I watched this officer open the trunk of his police cruiser from a window inside the building and open a can of wet dog food. He then filled a water bowl on the edge of the vacant lot. The dog slowly walked over to eat and drink by the edge of the lot. The officer (David Avalos) then fed him a bowl of dry dog food.

The appraiser finished his inspection, so I turned the lights off and locked the building up.

I walked over to watch this kind man feed and talk to this stray dog. I was filled with emotion. I love animals and especially dogs. I have two little dogs. He named him Dakota. David had not yet won Dakota's trust and could not touch him.

While talking with David, I found out that he came to feed Dakota twice a day. I asked, "What about your day off?" "I come and feed him every day," he said. I was totally taken aback. Wow, what an impressive man with a big heart I had met that day. I have never forgotten that day. Very few people would have taken the time for this stray dog.

There is a happy conclusion. David was able to catch Dakota and take him home before winter. Dakota is living happily ever after with David, his wife, and several other dogs. He is loved and is living the good life. Dakota's journey has its own page on Facebook.

Thank you for your kindness, David, and a memory I will never forget.

CHAPTER 62

Chichen Itza, Mexico

My friend Willa Conrad, former Toledo *Blade* classical music critic, invited me to go to Cancun, Mexico, and while there visit the Mayan ruins at Chichen Itza. The ruins are located on the Yucatan Peninsula about two hours by tour bus from Cancun. She knew that I had an interest in Indigenous cultures. The Mayan city was built in the 13th century. It was spectacular. The Mayans believed in human sacrifice. I saw a quarry where they pushed the honoree off a cliff to the stone floor below.

Besides the famous pyramid Kukulkan, there was a sports field with two parallel stone walls. Located about twenty feet up was a stone circle. The Mayan teams would compete by throwing a ball through the hole while on horseback. The winning team captain felt it was a great honor to win the match and then was sacrificed by death.

I was in my Harley persona while on this trip. One day a clerk at the hotel front desk suggested that I visit the mall nearby. An old Harley-Davidson motorcycle was on display in the front window of one of the shops in the outdoor square. So, I went. As I walked into the outdoor square, I spotted the shop he was referring to. A little boy came running up to me, excitedly pointing his finger at me and shouted, "Hulk Hogan is here, HULK HOGAN IS HERE!" I was wearing a red Harley tank top and a colorful bandana. He ran off and brought back about a half a dozen other little kids. They were all yelling, "Hulk Hogan, Hulk Hogan!" LOL My moment of fame!

They were selling handmade colored string bracelets and noticed I was wearing many on my right wrist. Yes, I made their day and bought a couple of bracelets from each one of them. I can image what they told their families when they returned home that day. "Mom, we saw Hulk Hogan today!"

That evening we went to the local disco. It was a cool round building with four open floors overlooking the dance floor. I was told that the first floor was reserved for VIP bullfighters. We went and thought we would be seated on one of the upper floors. I wore my "colors," the cool leather vest with all the patches and pins over a red Harley tank top. I also wore my red bandana, black Levi's, and sunglasses. The door attendant took one look at me and seated us on the first floor with the bullfighters.

CHAPTER 63

Compassion vs. No Compassion

In Chapter 61 I shared the story of Toledo police officer David Avalos's compassion for an abandoned dog name Dakota. Next, I will tell you a story of state highway patrol officer who had no compassion.

In 1994, I was the director of the Toledo Chapter Harley Owners group. We had a large group of people that shared a love for riding our Harleys. The big ride for the year was riding to Sturgis, South Dakota, the mecca for Harley riders from all over the world. It was a weeklong trip with many activities and great sights to see.

For many in this group it was going to be their first time on an overnight road trip. There were 20 bikes. The trip was about 1,250 miles and took two and a half days depending on the weather. We left Sylvania Harley-Davidson on Alexis Road at 8 a.m. on a Saturday morning, jumped on the Ohio Turnpike at the Maumee entrance on Reynolds Road and rode west towards Chicago. We rode in stagger formation. I was the road captain and was leading the group.

Somewhere near Bryan, Ohio, I rounded a curve in the road and noticed in my rearview mirror that I was missing a third of my group. I signaled to pull over and stopped my bike, dismounted, and asked if anyone knew what happed to the rest of our group. No one knew why they were missing. I could not see past the curve in the road. After about 15 minutes I became genuinely concerned and weighed my options for going back to find them. I was not sure how far it was to the next exit and felt it was not a good option because it would take too long. It was not a good option to ride ahead and find a cross over to turn around and go back the other way. I decided to turn my bike around and ride back on the berm as far to left and not right next to the driving lane. I did not get far when I saw an Ohio highway patrol car in the eastbound lane, lights on and the officer shaking his hand at me. I stopped right away. He crossed over the median, stopped his car behind my bike and started yelling at me for driving the wrong way. I tried to explain that this was an emergency and for all I knew one of my members was having a genuine problem. I was told to get in his car and produce my license, registration, and proof of insurance, which I already had in my hand. I got in his car and again pleaded my case. He checked my license and found I was not wanted, LOL, and had no warrants for my arrest. I said to him again politely, someone could be in trouble and may need assistance. You have my license, here are my keys would you go and check on them. He was not even listening. This officer had no compassion. Someone could have been hurt and he did not care. He was hell bent on writing me a ticket and giving me a lecture.

I offered to ride with him. No deal. He kept telling me that I was a law breaker by riding the wrong way on a one-way road and kept writing the ticket. I kept my cool even though I was seething inside. Just as he was finished and handed me the ticket the rest of the group rode by.

I got out of his car, turned my bike around and rode about a mile to where our group was parked. They had pulled off the ride because a newbie had not secured his bag very well; it fell off his bike and his clothes were strewn all over the highway.

On our second day, we were riding through Minnesota on I-90 when an unmarked "Special Police" car told me to pull over. No sooner was our group stopped than two more marked police cars pulled in behind us. Out came the drug-sniffing dogs. I told the officer that when you see the patch Harley Owners Group, we are the good guys sponsored by the HD factory. We were not outlaw bikers. I pointed out members of our group: "He is a lawyer, she is an artist, he is a funeral director, she is a magistrate, he is a police officer, I am a realtor ..." They found no drugs and let us go. Such BS!

We had an exciting time in Sturgis.

The first call I made when I returned home was to my attorney, Steve Newcomer. I told him what happened and sent him my ticket. I was not going to let this go. On the day of my court appearance, Steve and I rode together to the courthouse in Bryan, Ohio, on the Ohio Turnpike. We even rode through a rest area to make sure there were no one way signs. Folks, the Ohio Turnpike is not marked one way.

Guess what? The officer never showed up for court. The judge sent the prosecutor to check the turnpike to see if in fact it was not marked one way. He came back an hour later and agreed, it was not marked.

The judge dismissed the ticket. There are good and bad in every profession.

CHAPTER 64

Father Finnigan

I bought the mansion on Robinwood through Father Donavon, a Boston Catholic Irish priest. The Oblate Fathers of Mary Immaculate lived there for 40 years, 1937–1977. They were chaplains and teachers in the Toledo area. At one time there were nine priests that lived in the house. Their groceries were delivered, a house cleaner cleaned the house, and a cook prepared their meals. Mass was said every day at five o'clock in the third-floor chapel. Supper was at six o'clock.

The first time I went there, as I was viewing the first floor, I peered into the living room, which was behind two wide oak doors that had been added many years ago. There were nine reclining old gray rockers. Each had a pedestal ashtray and a single pole lamp. Each man had his own spot.

By 1977, their numbers had dwindled to four priests. It was time to sell their magnificent mansion. We purchased the home, closed on the property, and moved in August. Father Donavon and another priest moved back to Boston. Father Finnigan and another priest moved to Ann Manor apartment on the corner of Scottwood and Bancroft.

Father. Finnigan was a bit of a character. He spent many years as the chaplain at the Toledo Mental Hospital in South Toledo. Every other Friday he brought his paycheck to Father Donavon. He had a shot glass in a back pocket and his paycheck in the other. He traded a shot of scotch with Father Donavon for the paycheck. Father Donavon thought Father Finnigan spent too much time at the insane asylum, and it was rubbing off on him.

On Saturday of Labor Day weekend, the doorbell rang. It was about 12:30 in the afternoon. Father Finnigan was standing outside the front door. I opened the door and he said, "Mr. Murray, I am sorry to bother you. I was late getting to the liquor store, they closed at noon. You wouldn't happen some scotch, would you?" "It's Labor Day weekend and Monday's a holiday you know." I could tell he was upset. I invited him in and just happened to have a bottle in my liquor cabinet that my father had given me. I gave him the bottle. He blessed me and thanked me profusely. I never saw him again.

CHAPTER 65

Modeling Career

Michael Murray

Photo: Eric Hoppel

Height: 6' 2"   Suit: 44R
Hair: Gray   Shirt: 17 x 35 Tapered   *Traque*
Eyes: Hazel   Shoe: 11B   MODEL MGMT
Inseam: 33   (419) 244-7363

I n 1993, on a Saturday morning, my front doorbell rang at the mansion on Robinwood Avenue in Toledo. Lynn Clark introduced herself as my neighbor in the apartments across the street and the owner of the Traque Modeling Agency. She thought my home would make a beautiful place for a modeling shoot. I did not think long about it and gave her a quick answer ... bring them over. The following Saturday she came with three models and several photographers. Lights, camera, action!

The young man and ladies were cool to watch doing their poses and the photographers were very skilled. As Lynn was leaving, she said, "Michael, I need a man about your age to be the father of the bride in my wedding shows. Would you consider it?"

"I'm in," I said. The next thing I knew I was posing for my "Modeling Photo Card" aka Comp Card.

I really enjoyed modeling with the young men and woman both auditioning and performing in shows.

Besides playing the father of the bride, I also had opportunities as a runway model. This was all gratis, but it was fun, and I met some nice people.

I had one paid commercial shoot for a bank in Pittsburgh. I had to wear a suit that was two sizes to small and stand with my arms and legs outstretched. The headline in the ad was "First Bank is shrinking interest rates!" I was paid $125.

CHAPTER 66

Alaska or Bust 2013

T his was the greatest adventure in my lifetime both physically and mentally. My cousin Rick Fournier and I had not seen each other in over 25 years. His family had moved to the West Coast when he was a little kid. We reconnected on Facebook, and he was now living in Cleveland, Ohio. He brought me his new Harley to pinstripe. He came back two weeks later to pick it up. He and his lovely wife, Peggy, asked me to ride with them to Alaska in 2013. That was a big one on my bucket list. I had only ever met one other person who had made the ride. The ride was the adventure, heat, wind, rain and cold. A true test of confidence and endurance.

The plan was to leave on July 13 the following year. I was 68 years old and knew from my many years of riding experience that I would have to be in top shape physically to ride that far. In January, I started my weightlifting routine. I have a small gym in the lower level of my log home. Religiously, I worked out three times a week until bike riding weather. Starting in May I rode one hundred miles two nights during the week and 150 to 250 miles in one shot on the weekend.

My bikes were older and had many miles on them. The last thing you want to happen is to break down. I rented a new 2013 HD Electra Glide Limited from Signature HD in Perrysburg, Ohio. I picked the bike up a week before we left so I could get used to it. It was a motorhome on wheels.

Peg and Rick rode up from their home in Columbus the night before. I prepared them a delicious meal and we went over our itinerary. They spent the night in my log home. We left on Saturday, July 13.

July 13: Wauseon, Ohio, to Eau Clair, Wisconsin, 545 miles. Ridiculously hot and slow traffic through Chicago.

July 14: Eau Clair to Jamestown, North Dakota, 441 miles. Rained most of the day.

July 15: Jamestown, North Dakota, to Regina, Saskatchewan, Canada, 415 miles. Wind, rain, four tornados in the storm.

July 16: Regina to Edmonton, Alberta, 510 miles, sunshine.

July 17: Edmonton to Dawson Creek (start of the Alcan Highway) to Fort St. John to Fort Nelson, British Columbia, 510 miles. Sunshine.

July 18: Fort Nelson to Watson Lake, Yukon Territory, 235 miles. Only half a day of riding. Afternoon and evening naps (the little dogs could not keep up with big dog) LOL.

July 19: Watson Lake to Haines Junction, Yukon Territory, 329 miles. In the mountains in the rain. The Alcan Hwy is a two-lane road. About 20 percent was under reconstruction. Gravel, potholes and treacherous in the all-day rain. We had to follow a pilot truck because only one lane was open.

July 20: Haines Junction, to Burwash Landing, Yukon Territory, 433 miles. Rained all day.

July 21: Burwash Landing, Yukon Territory, to Tok, Alaska, 218 miles. Rain, road was heaved and sunken. We were in the middle of nowhere.

July 22: Tok, Alaska, to Anchorage, Alaska, 316 miles. Smooth road and sunshine.

We rode 3,888 miles in 10 days. It was a challenge: wind and rain for four and a half days, riding through gravel roads in construction zones. Peg Fournier took 6,096 photos. WOW!

A few back stories ... Burwash Landing was an old resort built in the 40s. Wi-fi only in a waiting room, payphone in the lobby and very laid back on a scenic lake. Our leathers were soaking wet beneath our rain gear. I removed my wet clothes and laid them out to dry. It was chilly in my room. No heat. I looked all over for a thermostat and there was none. Strange, I thought. I pulled open the curtain on the back wall and saw a wood boiler in the backyard and no smoke from a fire. It was 6 p.m. I knocked on Rick's door and made him aware of the issue. He went to the front desk and found out they do not fire up the boiler until 10 p.m. He slipped the manager a $20 bill to fire it up early. Wi-fi and cable were shut off at 11 p.m.

This was the only restaurant on our trip that did not open at 6 a.m. The sign said open at 7 a.m. About 7:30 an older heavy-set woman in her bathrobe, hair in curlers, finally opened the door for breakfast.

Mile post 1093 Alcan Highway, Yukon Territory, Canada (The Alcan highway is marked by mile posts.)

Our first evening In Anchorage, we were invited to the home of a retired air force colonel friend of Rick's. I was telling him the story about Burwash Landing. He looked at Rick and said, "I told you not to stay there!"

The last two gas stops in the Yukon Territory were l05 miles and 110 miles apart. There was nothing in between, no homes, no buildings, and no cell service. At the last stop, I asked the clerk at the one pump station how cold it got here. She said, "We don't know, the thermometer only goes down to minus 40 Celsius." "How bad is the road up ahead?" I asked. ''You haven't seen anything like it!"

In one of the construction areas, the bridge was out which meant we had to ride down an embankment, cross a wet stony bottom and up the other side. OMG! We were on road bikes, not dirt bikes. I had never done this before. I prayed, as I was the first vehicle to cross. My bike weighed over nine hundred pounds. If I dumped, it ... oh my! I prayed some more and told myself if I start to lose it keep my arms and legs tight to my body, so I do not break any bones. I turned up my courage and guts gauge then turned and told Rick not to start out until I made it to the other side. We both made it across! Whew!

Once in Anchorage, we checked into a hotel, then went straight to the Harley dealer and made an appointment for early the next day to get our bikes serviced for the trip back. We were only staying for two days then returning. The adventure was the ride. After we dropped our bikes off the next day, Rick rented a car for a little sightseeing. We were gone an hour when Peg received a phone call that her mother was extremely sick in Spokane, Washington. Within an hour and a half, we had her on a plane to see her mom. That evening the Harley dealer had a car and bike show. There are a lot of cool wheels in Anchorage.

Rick and I left early on July 21st and rode four days to Edmonton, Alberta. We then split up. He went south to Spokane to be with his wife and mother-in-law, and I rode six days home solo.

It was a great trip. The Canadian Rockies are magnificent. We saw caribou, buffalo, a moose swimming in a lake, bear, wolf, and big horn sheep. The Canadians are very friendly, and we met some interesting people. Ask me if I would go again ... "Been there, done that."

A tip of the hat to my cousin Rick Fournier for planning a great trip. I had a wonderful time with Rick and Peg. Rick and I got along so well, he came back a month later and helped me re-stain my log home.

Total miles 8,001 in 22 days.

CHAPTER 67

Act of Kindness

In 2007, I was touring Buenos Aires, Argentina. My friend and tour guide, Andrea had planned to take me to a car show one day. She sent a message that something had come up and she could not go but wanted me to come to her house for coffee and she would see that I got to the show. I called her from my hotel lobby, and she insisted that I take a bus and she would meet me at the bus stop by her home. I said that I preferred to take a taxi. I was in a city of ten million people, and I did not speak the language. I did not want to take a bus. It was much easier for me to write down an address and show it to the taxi driver. She asked to speak to the door attendant. Next thing I knew he was walking me out the door, down the street and around the corner to a bus stop.

After coffee, Andrea walked me to another bus stop and told the driver where to let me off by the show. I arrived at the grounds of the show, there was a locked gate, and a security guard was turning cars and people away. He spoke no English and I spoke no Spanish. I did not know how to get back to my hotel. No taxis were around, and I was not sure which bus would take me to my hotel. The guard sensed that I was stressed and asked each car that he turned away if they spoke English.

Finally, a young man, (Maxi age 15) got out of his mother's car and asked if he could help me. I explained my plight. He saw the Ford GT logo on the shirt I was wearing and asked if I owned a Ford GT. Maxi was a gearhead. I told him yes and showed him a photo. He asked his mother to help me, and she offered to drive me to my hotel in downtown Buenos Aires, an hour and a half away. I was taken aback. It was so nice of Maxi and his mom (Monica) to give me a ride. The traffic congestion in Buenos Aires is unreal. Wall-to-wall cars. It is like driving through Chicago in rush hour. I also met Maxi's little sister Cami. This was a wonderful family to go out of the way and help a foreigner. I offered Monica gas money, but she would not take it.

Three months later I was back in Buenos Aires and met Maxi and his uncle. I brought him several gifts as thanks and sincere appreciation: a custom Ford GT shirt like mine, a FGT hat and a large poster of my car. We became friends.

I took the opportunity to share some wisdom with my young new friend. Those of you that know me have heard me say, "Life is about making dreams come true. If you can dream it, you can do it." I have lived by this my whole life.

We became Facebook friends and talk regularly. Maxi is an engineering student and works for Ford in Buenos Aires. His mother, father, sister, and I are family. Maxi's dream was to come to the USA and go to Cars and Coffee with me and he made it happen. He saved his money and paid his own way.

He came in 2015 and spent 10 days with me. Every day I took him to something that had to do with cars. I took him to see my friend's private car collections. David Martin and I took him to the Gilmore Car Museum. We went to the Henry Ford Museum. My friend Grant Browning gave him a tour of the famous Pratt & Miller Corvette race shop where he got to sit in the Le Mans winning Corvette and kiss the trophy. We went to several car shows including Toledo's Cars and Coffee. Casey Putsch gave him a tour of Genius Garage.

Maxi ate his first donut and had American fruit pie.

One Wednesday we met my daughter Amy Murray Sigurdson for lunch in Arrowhead Park. There were six food trucks. I promised Maxi all-American apple pie. After we ate our lunch, we walked over to the truck that advertised dessert pies. She only had chocolate pie that day. I explained to her that I promised my friend a slice of apple pie and I was disappointed that she did not have any and he would be going back to Argentina in a couple of days. She asked if I would bring him by her shop on Central Avenue the next day and she would make him a special pie. We stopped on the way home from Detroit. She kept her word and made him four small fruit pies. North American hospitality at its best and she refused payment.

In 2016, Maxi and his friend Javiito Valerga met the Fritz brothers and me in Sebring, Florida, to watch the famous 12 hours at Sebring international sports car race.

Maxi called me last night and said that he will compete in his first sportscar race on December 21 in his Ford Focus. (Another dream come true.)

My friend Floyd Wickman teaches us, "We get by giving."

CHAPTER 68

A Will to Survive

In 2011 Jerry Nemire called me. I had not seen or talked to Jerry for many years. "Michael, you lettered my first car and I'd like you to letter my last race car." Jerry went on to explain that he had been fighting cancer for seven years and did not know how much time he had left. He had purchased an AJ Foyt Silver Crown Sprint Car 30 years earlier, raced it a couple of years, then put it in storage. Jerry was being honored at Toledo Speedway with a "Jerry Nemire Appreciation Night" on July 1, a mere six weeks away. His family talked him into getting the Foyt car out of storage and restoring it. His sons, JD and Kenny, took the car apart and started the restoration process. John Spilker at Waterville Body Shop was repainting it the same color, poppy red, and it would be ready for me to letter by the weekend. John's work was perfect. I also had to do my finest lettering.

I was flattered that Jerry remembered me and honored to be asked to replicate the lettering on this famous historic AJ Foyt Car. For those of you non-racing fans, AJ Foyt won the Indianapolis 500 four times. He is a racing legend. He won at Indianapolis, the Daytona 500 and the 24 hours at Le Mans, France, just to name a few.

I went to Jerry's race shop to see my next canvas. Jerry had many photos for me to see the original lettering. I took the hood home and lettered it in my studio, went back and lettered the numbers in his race shop.

When I was finished, Jerry asked how much he owed me. I told him no charge. During my time lettering Jerry's prized possession, we became reacquainted. I met his family and felt a kinship with them as well. Jerry Nemire was an expert mechanic, outstanding race car driver, a tough task master and a warm, kind, humble man. I could not take money from a dying man who was making his last dream come true.

Jerry said, "No, no, I insist on paying you, you did an outstanding job and have put a lot of time in it." You do not argue with Jerry. Thinking quickly on my feet I told him that I would give him the family discount ... $200. He wanted to pay me more, but I am as stubborn as he was.

It was a thousand-dollar job, but to me it was not about the money. In life there is also physic income. I was paid many thousands of dollars in physic income just being involved with Jerry, his family, and friends that I met in 2011 and have spent time with them ever since.

In 2013, I started re-staining my log home. The job carried over into the next year. My home has a metal roof that is too steep to climb. I had to re-stain the sides of three dormers that were perpendicular to the roof. I designed a metal bracket that I bolted to the fascia board at the lower edge of the roof, so I could lay a 2 foot by 6 foot by 4-inch board across. I could then rest the legs of an extension ladder on the board and climb up to paint.

I made an exact pattern and took it to Jerry who was an expert fabricator and welder. He made the brackets for me and when I asked how much I owed him he said with a big smile on his face, "Michael, I'm going to give you the family discount, 50 dollars."

Jerry fought off the grim reaper until this past spring. He made the best of his last years. He chuckled each time he beat the grim reaper. Jerry left his mark in life. He was inducted into the Toledo Speedway and Fremont Speedway's halls of fame. He was an inspiration to everyone he encountered especially his grandson, Austin Nemire, who is following in his grandfather's footsteps racing a Sprint car.

I loved Jerry as if he was my brother.

CHAPTER 69

The Platinum Rule

The rest of the story. You have all heard of the Golden Rule, "Do unto others," but have you heard of the "Platinum Rule?" Neither had I until I went to a Floyd Wickman Master Sales Academy conference in Las Vegas, in the mid-nineties. Art Fettig, author, and motivational speaker, taught us the "Platinum Rule." Give anonymously. You give and do not tell anyone or take credit for your kind act. Just do it and keep your mouth shut, no bragging or telling.

In late April Jerry's doctor gave him sad news. No more chemo, another dose would kill him. Jerry beat colon and liver cancer for 14 years; he was either a walking miracle or only plain stubborn as a mule. Esophagus and bone cancer was about to do him in.

Tony Stewart and Jerry raced against each other for many years and were friends at the racetrack, Tony had expressed interest in buying the AJ Foyt Silver Crown Race Car that the Nemire family had had for over 37 years and lovingly restored in 2011. Jerry called Tony and they made a deal. Tony said he would send his dad

to pick up the car. Jerry was hoping that Tony would come with him, but Tony said he could not get away.

I was invited to stop over that day. As I pulled up to Jerry's home, Tony Stewart was parked in front of me watching his dad back their truck and trailer own the driveway. Tony wanted to surprise Jerry. As I walked down the driveway, I saw Jerry with several friends helping him walk from the house to his shop. When I walked in Jerry was in his wheelchair. Right behind me was Tony. What a surprise for Jerry. It was very emotional for Jerry as Tony gave him a warm hug. I was emotional, as were several others. Tony went out of his way to make Jerry's Day. Jerry and Tony sat together talking racing stories when Tony said, "Jerry, I have good news for you. Your car is going straight to the Indianapolis Motor Speedway Museum!" WOW! What an honor for the Nemire family.

After about two hours of "bench racing," Jerry said to Tony, "It's a long drive back to Columbus, Indiana, don't you need to get going?" Tony replied, "I'm not ready to leave yet." Tony stayed with Jerry for another three hours.

This was the greatest act of compassion I have ever witnessed. Tony the Rock Star (three-time NASCAR Champion, Indy Car Champion) took the time to make a dying man's day. What a humble, kind man to do what he did that day. Tony's publicist could have written a press release, and the reporters, photographers and TV would have come to record this. Tony gave anonymously, he practiced the Platinum Rule. Tony Stewart moved up to be my number one hero that day. I will never forget that day.

Sadly, Jerry died peacefully May 16, 2017 surrounded by his loving family. A couple of days later, his son JD called and asked me on behalf of his family to paint Jerry's number, "Sweet 16," on Jerry's coffin. I lettered Jerry's first race car, his last race car and now his last ride.

RIP (race in peace) my friend.

CHAPTER 70

Steelers vs. Oilers AFC Championship Game

I n 1979, a neighbor called and asked if I wanted to go with him to Pittsburgh on Sunday to watch the Steelers play the Houston Oilers in the AFC championship game. The winner would go to the Super Bowl. He went on to say that he had press passes and we would have the best seats in the house.

We left at 3 a.m. Sunday morning for the five-hour drive. I did ask on the way over how he was able to obtain press passes. He said that he created a bogus company, "Foreign-American Feature Service" and wrote for press passes to major sporting and entertainment events. He had business cards, letterhead and envelopes printed. This was before the internet, and no one checked him out.

We arrived and picked up our passes and went immediately to the press breakfast. Chefs dressed in white prepared our "cooked to order" eggs served with prime rib. I had never seen a breakfast buffet with so much delicious food. The pastry table was right out of a French bakery. I was in awe!

Besides our press passes they also gave us a red armband that allowed us to go down on the field before the game to take photos and interview the players. I took a 35mm camera and a tape recorder. LOL! I saw Toni Fritsch, the field goal kicker for the Oilers standing alone for a moment, so I went over and asked to interview him. He was a star "footballer" (soccer) from Austria, a mere 5'7" and left his mark in America. He had been the field goal kicker for the Dallas Cowboys at Super Bowl VI and helped them win it. It was a blast playing reporter.

During the national anthem, I was standing twenty feet from, Terry Bradshaw, Lynn Swan and Franco Harris. Some of the top players for the Steelers.

When it was half time, we went again to the press dining room for chili and hot dogs. Steelers won 34 to 5.

Five months later, the neighbor called again and asked if I was going to the Indianapolis 500-mile race on Memorial Day. I said no, but I was going to the time trials two weeks before the race. He asked if I would pick up his press passes. No problem, I would be happy to.

Don Fritz and I went to the Indy time trials, picked up the Foreign-American Feature Service press passes and for the first time had access to the pit and garage area. WOW! In all the years I had attended the race and time trials I never saw the inner workings of the garage area. We had a blast.

On the way home, we had a carpe diem (seize the day) moment. Why don't we duplicate these passes? At Indy, they used a bronze-colored plastic badge with a bas- relief pace car that was pinned through a white ticket in the shape of the State of Indiana. There was a large number at the top of the ticket that allowed security to see what areas of the track you were permitted to be in. We had Number 1 passes, which meant we could go everywhere.

We had to do this quickly because I had to deliver the passes to the neighbor. We stopped at Don's house and picked up a piece of his children's play dough and went to his shop. Without too much trouble he duplicated the bronze pin by pressing it into the play dough, mixed up a plastic compound and added bronze powder. I copied the white ticket by running it through the copy machine and then dry mounting it on a piece of heavier paper. We made six passes, dropped the originals off that evening and took four for our friends to the race two weeks later. I still get a laugh out of this story.

CHAPTER 71

Machu Picchu, Peru

I n 2012, my good friend Lissetthe Villarreal invited me to chaperone a group of high school students with the Toledo International Youth Orchestra on a trip to Lima, Peru. The highlight would be a tour through the Sacred Valley of the Incas and the famous lost city of Machu Picchu sitting high on a mountain.

As soon as we arrived and checked into our hotel, we were bused to the Lima Ministry of Music where about 75 members of the Lima Youth Orchestra were waiting for us. Our children and theirs had been pen pals for about six months. The chairs were set up, our kids took their places, violins here, cellos there, etc. Both groups had rehearsed the same music so both orchestras jelled. Wow! These kids were great.

I noticed two rows of six special needs children on either side of the conductor playing color-coded wooden xylophones. I was intrigued. I have been to many orchestra concerts before but never saw special children as members playing an instrument. I was really impressed with their musical talent.

Lis asked me to say a few words when the concert was over. I was not prepared. "But I don't speak Spanish," I told her. "Don't worry, I'll translate." I said to the conductor the only words that came to mind, "You give children life and parents hope." I truly felt this in my heart. I have never see these combined musicians playing music in the USA.

I went around the room complimenting the musicians, getting my picture taken with them, and shaking hands. A small special needs woman named Catterine Vasquez, wanted her picture taken with me. I gave her a hug. She took my hand and walked me over to anyone that had a camera. She wanted our picture taken so she could hug me repeatedly. Catterine loved my warm hugs. She was so sweet; she brought tears to my eyes. I bet she hugged me six times. She was so precious. Her mother told me that Catterine was an actress, and a dancer.

That evening, Catterine and her mother, Elizabeth, came to the concert we played with another youth orchestra at a private school in another part of the city. (Lima has a population of 8.4 million.) She and her mother took a two-hour bus ride, so she could see me again. I made a new friend.

After this performance, we were guests at a cookout at our host's home with their kids, our kids, and many parents. They rolled out the red carpet for us. I was asked to sit at a table with teenagers, so they could practice their English on me. I asked about the special needs children playing in the orchestra. They said that in Peru, "All children have the same opportunity." This was profound. If only this was practiced in the USA.

Catterine and I became Facebook friends. She tags me regularly with photos of her performing.

One time she wrote me said, "Michael, do you think I'll ever find love?" I wrote back and said, "There is someone for everyone."

CHAPTER 72

Neighborhood Troublemaker

The Murray family grew up on Nicholas Street in South Toledo between South and Spencer Streets. There were eight of us, Ann, Jim, Michael, Terry, Mary, Patty, Bill, and David. My little brother Bill reminded me of this story. Big brother Jim and I were in our late teens. Our garage was behind our house. You had to drive down the alley to get to the garage. Most of the streets in my neighborhood in South Toledo, Ohio had alleys between the streets. One day Jim and I were washing his car when this 10–12-year-old kid name Dean Watkins aka "Deano" came along and threw dirt and stones at Jim's car. Deano lived on Lodge Street, which also backed up to our alley. He was a little neighborhood troublemaker. Deano then took off running down the alley, ducked between two garages and disappeared. We could not catch him. A week or so later, Jim and I were again working on our cars in the alley. This time little Deano, came about two houses away from us in the alley and started taunting us, daring us to catch him. Again, he ran down the alley, ducked between two garages and disappeared. Now we were pissed.

Third time's a charm. We caught the little AH and dragged him back to Jim's car, opened the trunk, picked his squirming ass up and put him in it, shut the lid and took him for a ride. I mean we took him for a ride ... up one alley and down another. The alleys were not paved so needless to say ... he had a BUMPY ride. We aimed for the potholes and made sure his ride was unforgettable. His little ride lasted about 20 minutes. We went back home and opened the trunk. He was white as a sheet. The kid got the message to not mess with the Murray brothers. I do not remember ever seeing him again.

Years later he worked with brother Bill at Promedica and was still talking about that ride in the trunk. He died in 2010.

CHAPTER 73

Heritage Trip to Ireland 2015

In September 2015, Ann, Jim, Michael, Mary, and David Murray along with Dave's wife, Marty, and Jim's wife, Mary Ellen, went on a family heritage trip to Ireland, the home of our ancestors. Ann and Jim had been working for 30+ years doing research on our family history. My father had saved a letter from his great Aunt Grace, written on June 23, 1925, which gave the name of the cemetery and the exact location of our great, great, great, great grandfather's tombstone.

"The family graves are in view of the steeple of Kenneth Cemetery. Opposite the third window of the protestant church (St. Bartholomew) that is built in the cemetery, across the carriage drive on the fifth line of graves. South of the church. It has a tomb stone of solid limestone, circular shape with the Murray name on it."

We found it located behind a newer stone that was placed 50 years ago. It was hard to read because it was weathered (no date but about 1800) and close to the new stone. We "selfied" it, so Dave could piece it together after we returned home. We also found the house of our great, great grandfather Denis Murray who immigrated from Dunmanway, Ireland, County of Cork in 1855 to Wheeling, West Virginia.

My sister Ann and I sat on a bench in the quiet cemetery and enjoyed thinking about all the history that was buried here. There were mass graves for the many that died in the potato famine from 1845 to 1850. The British let one million out of a total population of eight million people starve to death.

Ireland is a beautiful country and is truly the Emerald Isle. We flew into Dublin, toured a day then drove south to the small town of Dunmanway in the county of Cork about four hours' drive southeast of Dublin. We visited the St. Patrick's Catholic church, which was the parish of our ancestors.

Our tour guide in Dublin asked if there was anything we wanted to see besides the places he had chosen for us. My younger sister Mary wanted to visit the home of Mother McCauley, the founder of the Mercy Order of Nuns. Sisters Mary and Patty graduated from McCauley High School in Toledo. My sister Mary was incredibly special; she had a hard life. Her dream was to become a nurse but was told by the nuns at McCauley that she was not smart enough to pass chemistry. Mary passed and went on to become a nurse, which was her lifelong profession. When my parents were elderly and went to assisted living, Mary was the floor supervisor at Lutheran Village in Holland, Ohio, and took care of them until their deaths.

We arrived at the Historic Home of Mother McCauley about 4:30 in the afternoon and saw the sign that said closed at 3 p.m. Our tour guide knew the importance to Mary, so he went and rang the doorbell. A sister answered so he explained the significance of a tour for just Mary. The Sister agreed to give Mary a tour. It was the highlight of my sister's trip. Mary had never traveled before and seldom took a vacation. This trip and seeing the McCauley home was one of the brightest moments in her life.

My dear sister Mary passed away a year ago. We all miss her and think of her often. She was a saint.

CHAPTER 74

My Career as an Auctioneer

In 1998, it was time to sell my historic mansion in the Old West End. I was a VP at the Danberry Company. For several years, I watched more people selling their homes at auction and it intrigued me. In ordinary real estate sales, one negotiates down from an asking price. At auction you negotiate up. There is no ceiling. I did not know what my home was worth. An auction would give me the answer. My home sold at auction for the highest price ever paid for a home in the Historic Old West End. In those days people thought if you were selling your home via auction, you were in financial trouble. I laughed all the way to the bank. It was the first home to sell above $300,000 in the Historic Old West End.

In 2000, I joined the Pamela Rose Auction Company. I became an auctioneer. It was one of the best moves in my life. Good opportunities rarely come along. I have always had good street smarts and recognize future trends. "The greater the risk, the greater the reward." I was 56 years old; I had the best job you could have in real estate in this area at The Danberry Company, but I was bored. Pam gave me the opportunity to use the skills I had developed over 27 years as a realtor and broker. Pam and I are good friends and work well together. I am seventy-three, in good health and have no plans to retire. My career is fun. Why retire? I have plenty of freedom to come and go and I love Pam as my little sister.

Pam is a world champion auctioneer. My job is that of the project manager. I/we meet the client, sign the contract, and manage the auction from start to finish. I rarely call the bid except at benefit auctions. We have a very experienced team that are experts in marketing and managing both small and large auctions and they are wonderful people to work with. In 2009 we sold a home in Bloomfield Hills, Michigan, for $4.95M (to bid, you had to bring a bank check for $200,000; we had 20+ bidders). That same year we liquidated the Roger Dunbar Estate for $22M and liquidated all the contents in the Dana World headquarters on Dorr Street. We auction land, commercial and industrial property, personal property and give freely of our time to raise money for charities.

There is a new challenge every day. I like the fact that we are in and out of a job. Sign it up, market it, auction it and move on to the next auction.

In 2005, my friend Keith Knecht asked me to organize and auction pinstriped panels at the Detroit Autorama, the largest hot rod show in the mid-west. Over one hundred artists came from all the over the country and donated their art and time to raise funds for Rainbow Wish Connection, a Detroit charity. The first year we did seven auctions in three days and raised over $20,000. As the years went on, the art auction became so popular that we did 12 auctions over the three-day weekend. That annual auction still goes on today although I am no longer involved.

CHAPTER 75

24 Hours at Le Mans, France 2016

Bill Ford CEO and I

T he Ford Motor Company won their first 24-hour sports car endurance race at Le Mans in 1966. Fifty years later they went back to Le Mans and won it again.

In the early '60's Henry Ford II had a deal with Enzo Ferrari to buy Ferrari. At the last minute, Enzo reneged. You do not embarrass Henry Ford. He came back to America and told his engineers to build a car to beat Ferrari at the most prestigious sports car race in the world, the 24 hours at Le Mans. Ford succeeded in 1966 after several failed attempts with a mid-engine sports car named the GT 40. It was only 40 inches tall and ran a NASCAR 427 Ford engine. Ford swept the first three places and blew Ferrari's doors off. Ford was the very first American car to win at Le Mans. They went on to win the race four years in a row and rubbed Ferrari's nose in it. I was 22 years old and was racing my 1966 Shelby GT350 Mustang at the time. We only received our racing news in a weekly paper named *Competition Press*. I had mine air mailed, so I received it on Friday's five days after the weekends racing events. There was no radio, TV, newspaper or internet coverage in those days. I lived for my Ford racing news each week. I was an avid Ford fan. I loved the Shelby Cobras, GT 350s and closely followed the GT 40 program.

In 2016, The Ford GT Forum sponsored at trip to Le Mans to see the return of the Ford GT and hopes of winning again on the 50th anniversary of Ford's historic win. My friend Don Fritz came along. Don was the engineer on my race cars in the 60s and early 70s. We have had a great 50+-year friendship.

Disaster struck almost immediately when we were taking the train from the airport to the hotel. A pickpocket lifted Don's wallet and got his money, credit cards and passport. It was a nightmare getting a new passport.

We rented a car and made the four-hour drive to the beautiful small city of Le Mans, France. The French countryside was magnificent to see. I found a small apartment through Airbnb about 10 miles from the racetrack. The ad read one bed and a couch. LOL the bed was a futon, and the couch was a love seat! The apartment was clean, the sleeping was tight (butt to butt), but we managed.

The Ford hospitality was second to none. We had special parking with rides to the Ford hospitality centers. The main building was about 20,000 square feet on two floors overlooking the racetrack at the pit entrance. They brought in a Michelin chef to prepare our meals for three and half days. Sit down meals, no paper or plastic. We went first class. Bill, Henry III and Edsel Ford were with us for the weekend. They could not have been more gracious. The food was superb and the French deserts ... oh my!

About 100 yards away were the four Ford garages along the pit lane with a viewing area above and more food and drink. They provided a golf cart ride to get to and from. I was in Ford gearhead heaven!

We watched the start of the race above the Ford garage on the main straightaway. There were several hundred thousand people at the race. It reminded me of Indy 500 size crowds. Golf carts shuttled us around the track to different viewing areas. Saturday evening, we took a helicopter ride above the racing. Incredible views!

Ford was in second place throughout the night and finally moved into first place with 3 hours and 46 minutes left in the race. They crowd went crazy as we watched them pass for the lead. They held the lead and won their class over the second place Ferrari. We also finished third, fourth and ninth with our other cars. We watched the finish in the main hospitality building. Ford personnel passed out Ford flags and everyone was going crazy. Yelling, screaming and waving their flags! It was so emotional for me to be there; I could not stop crying. It was one of the greatest moments in my life!

Champagne was passed for everyone as Bill Ford addressed the crowd.

We were walking through Charles de Gaulle airport outside of Paris for our return home. Security personal came rushing towards us yelling, "Security alert, security alert, everyone outside!" We were close to an outside exit and got out quickly. Close by was a large concrete pillar we hid behind in case a bomb went off. Here came the military in full dress combat gear, AK47s and all. After about 45 minutes the all-clear was given. Someone had left a bag unattended in Air France ticket counter. Whew!

When I returned home, I wrote thank you letters to Bill and Edsel Ford telling them that I was there in spirit in 1966 and enclosed a photo of me and my 1966 Shelby GT350. I thanked them for a most memorable racing experience to be there in person and see their historic return and win. They wrote back and thanked me for coming. Bill Ford said I bled Ford blue.

CHAPTER 76

Marla and Scooter

In the mid 90's when we were getting the Toledo Chapter Harley Owners Group (HOG) up and running, there were a dozen or so motorcycle clubs in the Toledo area. Most would have an annual event like a motorcycle rally or a hog roast. Our chapter put on a charity bike show at the mall in February. "Come to our event and we'll support your event."

I met a person named "Biker Bob" who rode with a one percent group called the Roadmen. One percenters were not exactly members of the Outlaw Motorcycle Club but lived on the edge. For them to have the letters MC on their colors (vests), they had to wear a patch, "Support your local Outlaws." Toledo has an Outlaw chapter. Ohio is an Outlaw state except for a lone chapter of Hell's Angels in Cleveland.

The Roadmen invited our HOG chapter to a lobster roast at their clubhouse in North Toledo. About 20 of us went. I was standing in line next to my friend Kelby Marlett (ATF agent) and noticed the man with the tongs pulling a lobster out the pot of boiling water. His shirt rode up and we could see his pistol tucked into his pants. Kelby looked at me and said, "We're out of here by dark."

It was a beautiful summer night; a band was playing hard metal music when I noticed an attractive woman sitting alone on a picnic bench. She had rings on every finger, many bracelets, six pierces in each ear and several tattoos. I asked who she was and was told that she was a famous photojournalist with *Super Cycle* magazine named Marla. Larry Flynt (*Hustler* magazine fame) owned *Super Cycle* magazine.

I introduced myself to Marla and after some conversation I found out that she was only paid $500 a week and she had to pay all her expenses such as gas, repairs, meals and lodging as she cruised across the country going to 1 percent biker parties. Her job was to take photos at the parties, especially the wet T-shirt (wink, wink) contests that these groups held at midnight.

She was beating around the bush looking for a spare room to sleep in. If not, she would pitch a tent for her and her dog Scooter to sleep in behind an abandoned gas station. Well, I just happened to have a home with nine bedrooms including a guestroom with a private bath.

This led to a great friendship. She was a true Canadian gypsy, never married, no kids and did not want any roots. She made friends all over the country that she would stay with as she was going to photographic assignments at biker parties. She stopped by several times a year sometimes announced and sometimes I pull in my driveway and her bike was parked there. She stayed up all night writing her stories then sending them to Santa Monica, California, and sleeping all day. There was a mailbox at the corner where she would drop an envelope containing her film canisters and send them to California. She was not a free loader. She cooked, baked and did my laundry, then would be on her way. She was a great friend.

Sturgis, South Dakota is mecca to Harley riders. Bikers would come from all over the world to attend this annual event. Marla and *Super Cycle* magazine annually hosted a hog roast at the Flying V Ranch in Newcastle, Wyoming. It was scenic ride through the Black Hills National Forest ... except at night in the rain. OMG!

She asked me one year if I would lend a hand using my culinary skills at her party. I was going anyway so why not. I stopped at my Harley dealer on my way out of town. Big Jim saw me and asked if I heard about Marla. "No, what's up?" She was killed in a motorcycle accident on Route 6 in Connecticut the day before. She was an excellent rider with over 50,000 miles a year of experience. She must have been distracted, crossed the center line and hit a semi head on. Scooter, her dog, rode on the back seat and survived. I was devastated. She was a dear friend and I think about her often.

CHAPTER 77

Vietnam 2014

Trieu Hai Li on Flower Street in Ho Chi Minh city, Vietnam

I f you invite me, I come. A friend I met on Facebook invited me to travel to Ho Chi Minh City in South Vietnam to see their lunar new year celebrations. I love travel and am interested in different cultures. This was an unforgettable trip.

In downtown Ho Chi Minh City, they block off three city blocks and build the most beautiful floral arrangements that are displayed for a week. The theme when I was there was the year of the horse. Their displays reminded me of the spectacular Rose Bowl parade floats. People come from all over for to see this spectacular display. Many wear their traditional clothing.

It is also a time to honor their deceased elders. My host family had a shrine in their home to the husband/father who died 12 years earlier. On New Year's Eve, his life was celebrated. They prepared his favorite meal and give him gifts of (paper) gold, silver and new shoes. They prayed and burned incense. At the conclusion, the paper items were placed in a can, carried outside and burned, sending the gifts to him in the hereafter.

They also believe that the first male that crosses their threshold in the new year of their home will bring them luck. That was I.

My host's mother invited me to go to her family's celebration in Danang. She is one of eight. In her family home were shrines to her father and grandfather. The whole family gathers, about 80 people. Monks in saffron robes come and conduct the ceremony. They sing, they chant, they pray. At the conclusion, a feast is held.

The next day, the family takes a large tour bus to the cemetery. The graves are built above ground. The casket is entombed in ceramic tile with a hood over the front and top of the head. A picture of the deceased and an inscription is attached at the head of the tomb. In the center is a flower bed. When we arrived, the family tomb was washed, fresh flowers planted, and the ceremony began. Incense was burned, prayers were said and placed in an urn in at the front of the tomb. Each person then placed a stick of incense in the loved one's incense cone and of all his neighbors' as well. They believe that all the spirit neighbors are friends. We repeated this at three different tombs. The Vietnamese have profound respect for their elders.

While in Danang, we toured a Buddhist temple on top of a mountain at a tourist area named Ba Na Hills. The temple is hundreds of years old. It is the longest tram ride in the world up the mountain. We went back into the city for supper. While waiting for our food to arrive, a military man and his family came in. He was dressed in camo and wore a beret. He noticed me and nodded; I nodded back. I went over and introduced myself and shook his hand. He did not speak English, so his children translated for him. He was a helicopter pilot in the Vietnamese army.

I noticed the food had arrived at my table, so I said goodbye, shook hands and walked to my table. About five minutes later I saw him walking towards me holding a silver tray with two glasses of beer. I do not drink but I knew I would insult him if I did not chug a beer with him. I leaned over and whispered to Trieu that she may have to pick me up off the floor in a few minutes. I stood, accepted his gift, clanged the glasses and chugged the beer like a pro. It was weak beer.

This was my first visit to a communist country. In every city, town and village there was a loudspeaker system. They wake up and put you to bed with communist propaganda. It was very annoying.

In Vietnam I was treated royally. The country is one of the most beautiful I have ever toured, and the food was delicious.

CHAPTER 78

Batman and Robin

I met Greg Knott "Batman" and his sidekick Gary Miller "Robin" when I moved to the Old West End (OWE) in 1973. Greg was one of my favorite neighbors and characters. A little background on Greg. Do you remember the urban legends, the headless motorcycle rider in Elmore, Ohio, and the werewolf train conductor in Woodville, Ohio? Greg was the train conductor who wore werewolf hairy hands and a head mask back in the day around Halloween each year. He created quite a stir with his outfit. It made all the newspapers. When I met him, he was a fellow realtor who also lived and worked in the OWE. He was the president of the OWE Association and helped me organize the OWE Security and Block Watch program in 1981.

There are two parts to this story. Part 1: One sweltering summer night, my wife and I were sleeping in a middle bedroom in the mansion on Robinwood Avenue. She woke me up about 1 a.m. and said, "Do you hear that?" *Click, click, click* … Sounded like a bumper jack to me. We got out of bed and went in the front bedroom window facing Robinwood. More *click, click, click* … four kids were stealing the wheels off a big old four-door Cadillac across the street from our house. I quietly asked her to go and call the police.

KABOOM, they had two wheels off and kicked the jack out of the way and the car hit the ground! The sound of that Cadillac hitting the ground could have awakened the dead! Two kids started pushing the two tires north down Robinwood towards Virginia Street. The other two kids started working on the front wheels … *click, click, click.*

Part 2: Batman and Robin could not sleep on this sweltering summer night, so they were out sitting on their screened porch on the fourth-floor apartment building on Robinwood, one house north of Virginia Street drinking a beer. They noticed a car pull up across the street at the corner of Virginia and park; four kids got out and started walking down Robinwood in my direction. Batman knew they were up to no good, so he and Robin got dressed and snuck across the street and stealthily snuck up on the getaway driver who had fallen asleep behind the wheel.

Part 1 (continued): The police car came flying around the corner, lights off; two cops got out of the car, one kid took off running with an officer in pursuit and the other slid under the Cadillac. I hollered out the window, "He's under the car!" The police officer grabbed him. We got up, got dressed and went out the front door. There were three sets of red flashing lights at the corner of Virginia where all the action was.

Part 2 (continued): Batman was not going to let the getaway car leave the scene. He took an icepick and quietly snuck up on the passenger side and poked a hole in the side wall. The driver never stirred. They then hid in the bushes and when the two kids came running down the sidewalk with the stolen tires Batman and Robin swung into action. (BTW Batman and Robin were two men of short stature.) They each grabbed a kid, stuck a finger in their backs and told them to hit the ground. They then sat on them pretending they had guns poking them in the back.

Three police cars converged on the scene. By the time we got there, four of the five thieves were handcuffed and in the back of the police cars awaiting their ride to the Graybar hotel.

I congratulated Batman and Robin who were chortling with glee telling us their story. I loved these two crime fighters. What a story! I was ready to go home and go back to bed. One bad guy was not happy in his cramped quarters in the backseat of the police car. He was crying and screaming like a baby trying to kick out the back and side windows of the police car. I walked up and shined my flashlight in his face and said, "Crime don't pay in the OWE MF, pass it on!" He shut up.

Greg Knot was a legend in the OWE. He died accidently on January 10, 2010. His friends and neighbors thought so much of him that we started a collection and purchased a memorial bench in his honor that is resting in the OWE Arboretum at the corner of Robinwood and Delaware Streets. I will never forget his mischievous smile.

CHAPTER 79

Ron McCance

As we take this journey through life, we meet people along the way. Some stay as acquaintances and some stay and grow as best friends. I met Ron back in 1974 when I lettered his Ford F250 pickup truck he had just purchased. We hit it off then and our friendship grew throughout the years. We like to say that we are brothers from another mother.

Ron has spent most of his life in the building trades as a carpenter, millwright and general contractor. I lettered his "Kanwill Construction" van in 1979. Kanwill means "Can and will get 'er done."

He is also an accomplished musician. If you can sing it, he can play it on his guitar.

Ron and his sweet wife, Carol, built their log home from scratch right down the lane from me. They cut down the pine trees, dried the logs, stripped the bark, built the wood foundation, and lived in the basement for eight years while raising the logs and doing the finish work. Their home is most unique, and a work of art. Ron's artistic talent can be seen throughout the house. There is a tree in the center of the house that he built the steps around to the upstairs.

When we started the Toledo Hog Chapter in 1993, Ron was a charter member. The HOG chapter wanted to put on motorcycle shows at the Franklin Park Mall. Ron was able to open that door to a run of 18 years in a row where the HOG chapter raised over $600,000 for Jerry's kid's and MDA. Of course, it helped that he oversaw the maintenance department at the mall during that time.

We have traveled all over the country together, riding side by side. Our favorite trips were to the Pine Ridge Indian Reservation, with side trips to Sturgis, South Dakota, and the Rolling Thunder ride on Memorial Day to Washington, DC, and Bike Week in Daytona Beach, Florida.

We also shared a of love of Native American culture. Harley riders are just big boys playing dress-up. Many winter Sunday evenings were spent sewing our deerskin shirts and vests and adding intricate bead work on my dining room table.

I will never forget the time we rode home from the Lima, Ohio flat track races on a hot July night. It must have 80. degrees at 11 pm. Here we were riding side by side on Interstate75 for about 80 miles in Harley tank tops. Perfect night, perfect ride for two brothers (from another mother).

After many trips in South Dakota, we settled on renting small log cabins in Hot Springs, South Dakota about 50 miles south of Rapid City and a short ride to Red Shirt Table at the Pine Ridge Reservation. There is a bar in Hot Springs, South Dakota named the Vault. During "Bike Week," they held an event where motorcycles raced through the bar. The start line was at the front door. Left turn, right turn, right again down the hall and out the finish line side door. The patrons inside were cheering us on. Ron won first place in 1998. He is one crazy dude and that is why I love him!

CHAPTER 80

Last Call

One day, I received a call one day from Jeff Smith. He wanted to know if I could hand letter an urn. I said, "Of course I can." "What material is the urn made of?" "Stainless steel," said Jeff. *Mmm,* I have never seen a stainless-steel urn." "It's a pony keg," said Jeff.

Oh my, I knew there had to be a story. 'What would you like me to paint on this urn?" "'Last call' and my monogram," said Jeff.

Jeff was born in Milwaukee, the beer capital of the USA. He was allergic to all milk, breast milk and formula. His mother took him to the doctor. "The doctor told my mother if she did not get some nourishment in me, I would die." He told her to add one third beer and two thirds water to a baby bottle and feed him.

Jeff went on to explain that he was dying of cancer and did not want a funeral. He wanted a party at his favorite bar for his family and friends.

I was in West Toledo a day later and stopped by to pick up the urn. Jeff greeted me at the door with a Pabst Blue Ribbon in his hand. I got the picture. He offered me a beer, which I politely declined. I do not drink alcohol.

I delivered his urn a couple of days later. He loved it. This was about three years ago. Great guy with a fun personality. I do not know what ever happened to him, but I never forgot him.

If you have left us, Jeff, I hope you are enjoying the hereafter where there is no last call. The heavenly bar is open 24/7.

CHAPTER 81

My Art Accomplishments Brag Page

The first time I went to the Toledo Art Museum, I was a 15-year-old first year art major at Toledo Central Catholic High School. I was in awe at the master artworks on display. I dreamed that someday my art would be in a museum. I am proud to say that today I have five cars on display or have been shown in five museums, and I pinstriped the oldest Ford known to exist (1903 #30), which is on permanent display in the lobby at Ford World Headquarters in Dearborn, Michigan.

#1. On April 14, 1931, the Twenty Millionth Ford rolled off the assembly line in Dearborn. It was restored by Deter's Auto Restoration in 2002 for display at Ford's 100th Anniversary and has been displayed at the Henry Ford Museum in Dearborn, Michigan.

Zora Duntov (father of Corvette Racing) 1974 Corvette, restored at ACI American Custom Industries in Sylvania, Ohio. It is the feature car at the Corvette Museum in Bowling Green, KY.

#3. 1940 Lincoln Limousine number 3 of 14, used by the Ford family, restored by Jim Blanchard, has been displayed in the Lincoln building at the Gilmore Museum in Hickory Corners, Michigan.

#4. "Irish" Jim McCune's Super Modified Race Car won 45 feature races in 1958/1959 at Fremont Speedway and is on display at their Hall of Fame Museum.

#5. AJ Foyt's USAC Silver Crown car restored by Jerry Nemire family and friends has been displayed at the Indianapolis Motor Speedway Museum and Sprint Car Hall of Fame Museum. Currently owned by Tony Stewart.

6. In 2013, I pinstriped the oldest Ford known to exist and is on display in the lobby at Ford Motor Company in Dearborn, Michigan. It was restored by Deter's Auto Restoration and High Point Restoration. I introduced myself to Bill Ford when I met him at the Le Mans, France 24-hour race in 2016. I had the photo open on my cell phone and asked him if he recognized this car. LOL "That's my car," he said. I told him that I pinstriped it. He became my new best friend for the weekend.

My parents said that I would starve as an artist. LOL

"If you can dream it, you can do it!"

This is my art legacy. I cannot wait to see what tomorrow will bring.

CHAPTER 82

My Ford GT

I n 2003 Ford announced that they were building a hundredth anniversary car that would be a remake of their most famous race car, the GT 40, the Ford-powered car that won the 1966 24 Hours at Le Mans, France, and won this famous race four years in a row. Wow, I had to get one. Dream big, take a financial risk, and go for it.

I taped a photo of the first picture I found on my bathroom mirror. I bought the first model and set it on my desk. Every day I dreamed. My bubble broke when reports came out that the Ford dealers were tacking on a $30,000, $40,000 up to $80,000 premium on the car. It would have been a real stretch for me to buy it at the list price of $157,000. Anything above put the car out of reach for me.

To sooth my bubble being burst, I flew to Florida and ordered a 2004 Back-Draft Racing Cobra. I always wanted a Cobra. Five months later I flew back and drove my new car home. It was a fun car. It turned heads whenever I took it on the road. It was loud and fast!

A year later, I received a postcard in the mail from Super Performance, a Cobra sports car aftermarket manufacturer. It featured a period correct Ford GT40 MKII clone and led you to believe that if you ordered it then (November) you could pick it up in the spring. The price was only $130,000. My boss came in my office, and I showed her the picture of my new car. She said, "I want your Cobra." Sold! I then called Super Performance and told them I wanted to order the GT40. Much to my chagrin, they told me the postcard was a marketing exercise to evaluate the market to determine the demand and the car would be at least two years out from production.

Boy, was I upset. The next day, my good friend Greg Armstrong called and asked if I would like a ride in the new Ford GT with one of the chief engineers, Jay O'Connell, who was a friend of Greg's in the Porsche Club. The next day I am riding with Jay in a new Ford GT doing 130MPH on the Southfield Freeway in Dearborn, Michigan.

I shared my tail of woe. He suggested that I search on Edmonds.com and look for cars that dealers in the north would be sitting on until spring. Clever idea. I took his advice; it was Thursday morning, and my first choice was white with blue stripes. I emailed 12 dealers that had my color choice. The best price I found was $185,000. On Friday, I went with my second color choice, blue with white stripes. Third email I got a hit at a small dealership in Hemlock, Michigan. They wrote back and only wanted $6,000 over sticker. I waited until 4:45. It was a Friday, the best time to make a deal. I called the salesman, introduced myself and told him that I would pay sticker price, not a penny more and he had until 5 p.m. to accept or I would go to the next dealer on my list. Five minutes later he called and asked me when I was picking up my new car. Greg and I went the following Wednesday and drove it home.

My dream finally came true. "If you can dream it, you can do it."

The car not only fulfilled my dreams, but also made me a rock star! My friend Chris Ashworth aka Dt1Rockstar made a YouTube video that has over 1,573,533 (03/26/2022) views as of today and is still climbing.

I take it to cars shows on a regular basis. My car is usually the one that attracts the most attention. It has won many "Best of Show" awards and several loudest car contests (162 decibels). People follow me to take a photo. If I stop at the grocery store, there is a crowd looking at it in the parking lot. When I am getting gasoline, it draws a crowd.

Owning the car opened the door for me to go to Le Mans in 2016 as a guest with the Ford GT Forum.

It gets better … Ford has built a new Ford GT super car and will build 1,350 cars over the next five years. Only 600 will remain in the USA. I and 6,700 other people applied to Ford to buy one. I was chosen to buy one in 2019.

2019 Ford GT Vin K085 was delivered March 14, 2019, at Brondes Ford in Maumee, Ohio. It is one of one in this color scheme.

Here is the lesson … when you take a risk and reach for the sky, you never know how far it will take you.

CHAPTER 83

THE END

When I wrote my first story in October 2017, I had no idea I had 82 vivid stories stashed away in my memory bank. Sincerely, I thank each one of you for reading my stories.

You have also learned something else about me. I am extremely passionate when I set my mind to do something. I eat it, sleep it and drink it. It has been one of the keys to my fun, exciting and successful life. I believe if you are going to do something, jump in with both feet and do not quit until you succeed.

As a parting gift, I would like to share with you a few secrets of happiness and success that I have learned along the way. I share these secrets with at-risk teenagers at high schools and at Stryker prison for juvenile offenders. It is my ministry to help young people get a head start in life.

Never do less than you say you are going to do.

Always take the high road.

"Five years from today you will be the same person you are today except for the people you meet and the books you read." —Charles "Tremendous" Jones

"Do not whine and be grateful." —Og Mandino

Set goals then work to achieve them.

You get out of life what you put into life, take calculated risks.

Read every day.

You never know how far you can go until you go too far.

Why be ordinary when you can be extraordinary?

"The harder you work the luckier you get." —Richard Petty

Live by the golden and platinum rules.

"Begin with the end in mind." —Steven Covey

"There is nothing special about special people; it is what they do that makes them special." ---- Floyd Wickman

"We get by giving." —Floyd Wickman

If you can dream it, you can do it.

Love is the only thing you get more of by giving it away.

Michael